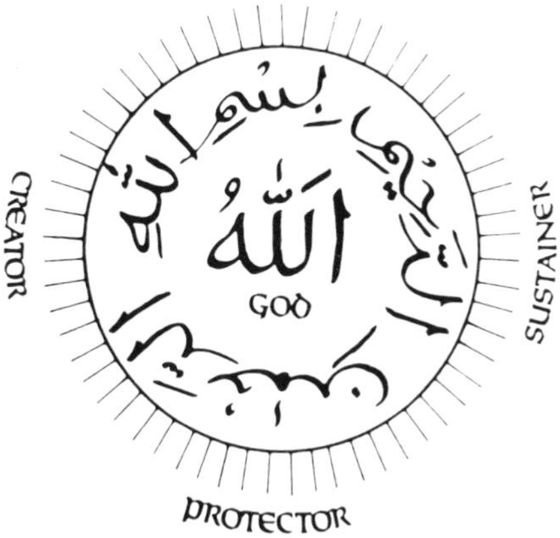

CREATOR
الله
GOD
SUSTAINER
PROTECTOR

ISLAM & WORLD PEACE
Explanations of a Sufi

REVISED EDITION

M. R. BAWA MUHAIYADDEEN

Foreword by
Annemarie Schimmel
Harvard University

The Fellowship Press
Philadelphia, PA

Library of Congress Cataloging-in-Publication Data

Muhaiyaddeen, M. R. Bawa.
Islam and world peace: explanations of a Sufi / M. R. Bawa Muhaiyaddeen ; foreword by Annemarie Schimmel – Rev. ed.
p. cm.
Includes index.
ISBN 0-914390-65-1 (pbk.) – ISBN 0-914390-68-6 (hc.)
1. Islam–Universality. I. Title: Islam and world peace. II. Title.

BP170.8.M83 2004
297.4'1--dc22

2004043208

Printed in the United States of America
by THE FELLOWSHIP PRESS
Bawa Muhaiyaddeen Fellowship

First Printing 1987
Second Printing 1990
Third Printing 1991
Fourth Printing 1995
Fifth Printing 1999
Sixth Printing 2001
Seventh Printing 2002
Revised Edition 2004

Muhammad Raheem Bawa Muhaiyaddeen

Editor's Introduction

Muhammad Raheem Bawa Muhaiyaddeen, may Allah be pleased with him, was an Islamic Sufi from Sri Lanka who dedicated much of his lifetime to instructing people on the true meaning of Islam and the path of Sufism. Though he himself was unlettered, the depth of his understanding of the Qur'an and the traditional stories of Islam has been recognized by Muslim scholars throughout the world.

It is appropriate that *Islam and World Peace: Explanations of a Sufi* should be his first book published posthumously, for during the last decade of his life, Bawa Muhaiyaddeen repeatedly expressed concern about the unfavorable image of Islam in the world today. He proclaimed an Islam of mercy and compassion, an Islam of peace and unity.

Opening with a plea that we must do more than just talk about peace, the book follows with a letter to world leaders, boldly calling upon them to unite. From there, the reader is guided to a view of the present day political crisis, then on to a Sufi application of the traditions of Islam, and finally to an esoteric understanding of the path of the innermost heart. Out of every page there emerges the wisdom of a contemporary mystic, blending the ancient oral tradition of Sufism with modern-day issues.

These talks, originally spoken in a mixture of Tamil and Arabic, were simultaneously translated into English, and later edited into a written format. For the benefit of the Western reader, the customary honorific phrases have not been used following the names of prophets and angels. For example, the phrase *Sallá Allāh 'alayhi wa-sallam,* God bless him and grant him peace, is traditionally spoken after mentioning the name of Prophet Muhammad. Since the reverence inherent in this phrase is evident within every page of the book, we hope that this omission will not offend anyone. For the reader familiar with Arabic, the translated Islamic terms have been footnoted. And finally, since there is no single accepted system for transliterating Arabic into English, we have selected the one recommended by the Library of Congress, which can be found in the glossary.

This book is a unique plea for peace and unity, and if God so wills, perhaps those who read it will find some guidance in the timeless wisdom of Bawa Muhaiyaddeen.

Karin Marcus
Executive Editor
Fellowship Press

Introduction

What We're Missing

On television we see lines of Islamic men bowing down, touching their foreheads to the ground, sitting back, standing up, kneeling, bowing again. What we may not see is that they're doing a form of prayer acknowledging unity, not political or religious solidarity with each other, but praising the mystery of oneness within all living things, all molecules even. That unity, which makes us want to bow in praise and surrender is true Islam. I met the essence of that in Muhammad Raheem Bawa Muhaiyaddeen.

"My brothers and sisters," he tells us in this book (pp. 129-130), "even though we have not yet seen God, there is no place where He does not exist. He is within every life. He is in the trees, the flowers, the fruits, and in the plants and shrubs and vines. There would be no flowers or fruits on a tree if His power did not exist within it. When we squeeze a fruit its sweet juice can quench our thirst and satisfy our hunger, because it has His power within it. The same intensity of sweetness exists within the ideals of Islam."

In these times, people in the West may have difficulty tasting that "intensity of sweetness," but it is there. It was there in Bawa Muhaiyaddeen's presence, and hopefully it will come through these words of his to readers.

So there's the unity and the sweetness. There is also the deep inward search. "...if you can know your own life and understand it, you will find the ocean of divine knowledge within you. You will find the Qur'an within you. You are the Qur'an; you are your own book. If you can study that book and reach the state of fully ripened knowledge, then you will be able to speak of its sweetness and know peace and comfort in your life." (pp. 126-127)

There is also a coolness and peace in Islam, like the coolness of the huge round pillars that hold up the Blue Mosque in Istanbul. They are filled with circulating spring water.

As-salaamu 'alaikum (God's peace be with you) is the greeting heard everywhere; I have come across an interesting etymology that I hope is true. In the 1840's sailors back from the slave trade routes in the English seaports of Bristol and Cardiff were heard exchanging the greetings they had heard among the slaves. "So long," one would say, and "So long," the other would answer. They were mispronouncing *As-salaamu 'alaikum,* the *salaam* part anyway. I love it when sacred traditions mix in a friendly way, so that when some good old boy in overalls in Thomson, Georgia backs his pickup out of the hardware store parking lot, and waves to the guys on the steps, what they are wishing each other is the peace of Islam. We know not what we do. So long.

Bawa Muhaiyaddeen advised that we should look within our religions and find where we meet. A child asked him once what she should say at school when they asked her what religion she was. The answer he gave can help us learn how to widen the boundaries of community until we all become one family.

> "Say, 'I am *Saivam* (a Hindu).' And if they ask you what *Saivam* is, say, '*Saivam* is purity.'
>
> "Then say, 'I am a Christian.' And if they ask you what Christianity is, say, 'I follow the pure soul.'
>
> "Then say, 'I am a Jew.' If they ask you what that means, say, 'It means...to be freed from all the things that enslave us in our life so we can reach that pure soul.'
>
> "Then say, 'I am Islam.' And when they ask you what Islam means, say, 'Islam is unity. *Lā ilāha illallāh.* There is nothing else other than God. You are Allah, You are God. That is the *kalimah.* You affirm that there is only one God and have firm faith in Him....My religion is purity. To become free and to become one family is Islam....'
>
> "Tell them, 'I am in a group that brings all people together in unity. God said that when we go to Him we must go as

one. I belong to a group that unites everyone, so I belong to all the groups.'" (*Why Can't I See the Angels?* pp. 73-74)

Here in 2002, our situation has gotten very simple and urgent: If we hold to what divides us into different religions, nations, and races, we will be encouraging the world itself to commit suicide. Read this book then, as Rumi tells us to read: Feel the presence inside the language, the healing and the compassion and the tremendous courtesy. *Adab,* courtesy and manners, is a deep quality in the Islamic and Sufi traditions. Francis of Assisi absorbed the Sufi gentleness. Thich Nhat Hanh and the Dalai Lama suggest that it is time for us to become conscious of our anger and not to act from there. Only more suffering comes from such discourtesy. We must sit down and talk with the great souls of other lineages, find where we agree and develop understanding when we cannot agree. We must protect and nourish each human life. As Bawa Muhaiyaddeen instructed:

"Make yourself aware, and by making yourself aware, you will make others aware. Don't waste your time. We have very little time left! We must say this silently with every breath,

Other than God there is nothing.
God alone exists.

"In this way we are in unity with the eternal One."

Love is the way this sense of unity says its truth. Love for every life form on this fragile blue planet, and in the eighteen thousand universes (!) too, that Bawa Muhaiyaddeen referred to with such grace and tenderness and humor.

Coleman Barks
July 24, 2002

Contents

Foreword

Among the great religions of the world, Islam is no doubt the one that is least known and least appreciated by the non-Muslim world. The recent resurgence of military and militant groups inside Islam has caused a renewal of feelings and sentiments that have been harbored for centuries and a new spirit of crusade against the only major religion that appeared in history after Christianity. This has caused many Western laymen and intellectuals to ask, "What do *'the Islams'* have in mind now? (A horrible form used by many instead of the correct term, *Muslims.*)

Real Islam is a deep and unquestioning trust in God, the realization of the truth that "There is no deity save God" and of the threefold aspect of religious life: that of *islām,* complete surrender to God; *īmān,* unquestioning faith in Him and His wisdom; and *iḥsān,* to do right and to act beautifully, because one knows that God is always watching man's actions and thoughts. For fourteen hundred years the Muslims have practiced these virtues, and the great mystics of Islam have taught them to millions of faithful who have survived the most difficult times, the greatest hardships because of their unshakable faith in the loving kindness of God, the creator, sustainer and judge of everything created.

Sufism, the mystical current inside Islam, developed logically out of the serious study of the Koran, according to Muslim belief the uncreated word of God, and of the constant direction of all faculties toward God. The Sufi masters taught their disciples that their duty is the fulfillment of God's will, not out of a feeling of duty but rather out of love—for could there be anything greater than the unconditional love which man offers his Lord? And in order to be able to love God and, through Him, His creatures, the heart has to be purified by constant remembrance of God and by constant struggle against one's lower qualities, the so-called *nafs,* which are, according to the word of the Prophet of Islam, "the greatest enemy of man." This struggle against one's lowly and base qualities is indeed the "greater Holy War," for outward enemies can disappear and are not as dangerous as the inner, satanic forces, which try to incite man into evil, disobedience, and forgetfulness. It is this "Holy War" which in the following pages forms the center of the teaching of one of the masters of Sufism in our day, Bawa Muhaiyaddeen, who hails from Sri Lanka and stands in the age-old tradition of wisdom and love.

The reader will learn from these pages, which are written, or rather recited, in a simple, almost childlike style, that the inner dimensions of Islam are very different from those which he usually associates with this religion; that there is a wealth of love, of patience, of trust in God, and, last but not least, of gratitude; for the qualities of patience in affliction and gratitude belong together. The true lover of God knows that even in affliction it is the hand of the Divine Beloved that he feels, and he trusts that whatever befalls him is for his best, for God knows what is good for the soul's growth and for the spirit's purification.

I hope that many people read the warm, loving words of Bawa Muhaiyaddeen and understand that indeed the words *islām* and *salām*—peace—belong to the same root and that a true understanding of the inner dimensions of Islam will help them to find peace for themselves, *inshā'Allāh,* God willing.

Annemarie Schimmel
Professor of Indo-Muslim Culture
Harvard University
Cambridge, Massachusetts

Preface

In the name of God, Most Merciful, Most Compassionate.

It is important in this present day that the children of Adam clearly understand the true meaning of Islam. We must know the value of its purity, of its peacefulness, its unity, its sincerity, its honesty, and the value of its conscience and justice and truth. We must know the greatness of Allah who rules over all this, and we must find tranquility in our lives, so that we will be able to guide others toward peacefulness.

To all those who have accepted Allah and His Messenger, Muhammad, with perfect faith, certitude, and determination[1]—before we can bring peace to all lives, before we can eliminate poverty, suffering, illusion, and disease in the world, before we can come to love every life as we do our own, we must first understand the value of absolute faith. That is the purpose of this book.

To have determined faith in Allah, the Almighty Lord,[2] to know Him and to bow down at His feet, to pray to Him and adopt His ways, to believe with complete certitude in His messengers, prophets, and angels, to carry out the commandments sent through them, to bring into our actions His three thousand gracious qualities and His ninety-nine attributes,[3] and to dedicate our lives to His service—this is the true meaning of Islam.

Islam is equality, peacefulness, and unity. Islam is inner

1. *īmān*

2. *Rabb*

3. *wilāyāt*

patience, contentment, trust in God, and praise of God.[4] One who understands this and puts it into practice will be a true believer. He will be Allah's representative; he will know Allah and His commandments and practice the explanations given through His revelations; in his own life he will demonstrate Allah's qualities, His actions, and His conduct.

We who claim to be in Islam must destroy all the evil qualities that arise within us. We must cut away and discard all that God discarded from Himself, all the differences that separate us from Him. We must remove all the thoughts that disrupt the unity of Adam's children, the unity of Islam. We must fight against the separations that grow within our bodies, sucking our blood like animals and demons.

With the wealth of God's grace and with the help of His messengers, we must wage a holy war against every one of the four hundred trillion, ten thousand evil qualities that come to destroy our good qualities. This holy war, this *jihād,* is not something that can be fought on the outside; our real enemies have been within us from birth. If we are true human beings,[5] we will realize that. Our own evil qualities are killing us. They are the enemies that must be conquered. We must control and subdue them and keep them in their place. We must show these animal qualities their true master, Almighty God,[6] and we must win them over and teach them faith in Him. That is the way of Islam, and that is what this book urges us to do.

Allah's perfectly pure qualities, His conduct, His ninety-nine attributes, and His three thousand gracious qualities have all been gathered together with His love and made into the treasure of *Īmān-Islām.*[7] Allah has given this gift of *Īmān-Islām* to the true believers, to those who have absolute faith, certitude, and trust. He has given this gift to the children of Adam so that they might receive

---

4. *ṣabr, shukr, tawakkul 'alá Allāh,* and *al-ḥamdu lillāh*

5. *insān*

6. *Allāh ta'ālá*

7. *Īmān:* absolute faith, certitude, and determination.
Islām: the state of absolute purity. See glossary.

the wealth of Allah's kingdom and live a life filled with peacefulness. He gave this gift in abundance to the prophets, so that they could help man to free himself from his enslavement to earth, gold, sensual pleasures, desires, thoughts, and attachments. And yet man is suffering and can find no freedom; he is a slave to so many things. He has no peace, tranquility, equality, or love. The children of Adam must release themselves from the bondage of this suffering.

If only man could acquire the wealth of Allah's love and integrity, the wealth of His beautiful laws, then he would never lack anything. That wealth is pure; it is the purity of Islam. If man had such inner wealth, he would never meet with destruction in this world or in the hereafter. He would be beautiful in both worlds. Allah has asked mankind to accept this, to find freedom, and to raise the flag of unity on the tree of love.

My brothers and sisters, in the name of Allah and Prophet Muhammad, please forgive me if there are any mistakes in what has been said in this book. People with wisdom know that it is important to correct their own mistakes, while people without wisdom find it necessary to point out the mistakes of others. People with strong faith know that it is important to clear their own hearts,[8] while those with unsteady faith seek to find fault in the hearts and prayers of others. This becomes a habit in their lives. But those who pray to Allah with faith, determination, and certitude know that the most important thing in life is to surrender their hearts to Allah. If the pond of the heart is full, then all creations can come and partake of its clear water. If it is shallow, then all those who come will stir up the mud and have nothing but dirty water to drink.

A fruit can only give the taste that it has within itself. In the same way, the children of Adam can only give what they have within themselves. If we have wisdom, others with wisdom will recognize that taste. If we have sweetness in our hearts, we will recognize that taste in others. If we can find truth, patience, and tranquility deep in our hearts, if we can find Allah and His Messenger there, and if we

8. *qalb*

can find unity among ourselves, then we will be truly exalted people. Unity, compassion, and truth are Islam. Let us realize this and live accordingly.

Let us constantly strengthen our faith, certitude, and determination. We must unite and live as one race, accepting that there is one God and praying together as one family in one gathering. This is the wealth of *Īmān-Islām.* God sent this gift to each of the prophets and finally gave it in completeness to Muhammad. The fundamental explanations of perfect faith were resonated to God's messengers, and they in turn shared them with mankind in the scriptures, in the traditions of the Prophet,[9] and in the Qur'an. There are very deep meanings to be found in these.

In this book, we are revealing to you only an atom of the value of Islam. The words we speak come from the little wisdom of this small man. Those with deeper wisdom may understand even deeper meanings. Such meanings will be seen with clarity by those who have Allah's divine knowledge[10] and His wisdom. If there are any mistakes in what has been spoken here, please forgive me. All the children of Adam, all who accept God and have perfect faith are one family. Therefore, please forgive me as you would forgive the mistakes of those in your own family. We are all in Islam.

Allah is sufficient for all. May His peace, beneficence, and blessings be upon you.[11] Amen.

---

9. *aḥādīth*

10. *'ilm*

11. *al-salām 'alaykum wa-raḥmat Allāh wa-barakātuhu kulluh*

PART ONE:
PEACE

سَلَام

Salām

Peace

This world is a pulpit upon which man preaches, and there is no end to this talk! For millions of years man has been speaking about peace, but he has not come forward to first find peace within himself.

EVERYONE IS SPEAKING OF PEACE

أَعُوذُ بِاللَّهِ مِنَ الشَّيْطَانِ الرَّجِيمِ بِسْمِ اللَّهِ الرَّحْمَٰنِ الرَّحِيمِ

I seek refuge in Allah from the evils of the accursed satan.
In the name of Allah, Most Merciful, Most Compassionate.

Brothers and sisters born in this world, please listen to this wonder! The heavens and earth have always existed in peace. The sun, the moon, the stars, and the wind all perform their duty in harmony. Only man, who lives on this earth, has lost that peace. He only talks about it. He gives speeches about establishing peace, but then he disrupts the unity and sets out to rule the world. Is this not a wonder? Such is the speech of man.

In this present century, man has discarded God, truth, peacefulness, conscience, honesty, justice, and compassion. Man has changed so much! Instead of searching to discover the three thousand gracious qualities of God, he has lost all those qualities and opened the way to destruction. He seeks to ruin the lives of others and to destroy the entire world. But the world will not be destroyed; the earth and the heavens will never be destroyed. Only man will be destroyed. Man, with all the various means of destruction he has discovered, will in the end destroy only himself. He is like a certain type of moth that is attracted to the glow of a flame, thinking it is food. These moths circle around and around the flame, until finally they fly right into it and die. In the same way, man plummets into evil actions, thinking they will benefit him. He sees evil as good, but the end result is destruction.

Never has destruction been so much in evidence as in the present century. Man has changed the concept of God, who is truth, and debased the meaning of man, who is wisdom and beauty. He no longer understands what a true human being really is. If man could rediscover who he truly is and then change his present self, he would know peace. Man says he wants to bring peace to others, but in order to do that he must first find it within his own life. How can anyone who has not found peace within himself hope to bring peace to others? How can a man who has no compassion, no unity, and no love within himself bring peace to the world?

One who has not found justice, conscience, honesty, and truth within himself will not find these qualities in others. One who has not found the value of patience within himself will not find it in others. One who has not understood his own state will not understand the state of others. One who has not strengthened his own faith in God cannot strengthen the faith of others or be strengthened by the faith of others. One who has not acquired good qualities cannot find them in others, nor can he teach them to others. If he tries, his work will be fruitless. How can a man who carries a water bag full of holes hope to quench the thirst of others? As long as he has not repaired his own vessel, he can never fill that of another man.

To understand this and to establish peace, man must first change the thoughts and qualities within himself. He must change his qualities of selfishness and avarice, his desire for praise, and his love for earth, sensual pleasures, and gold. He must stop thinking, "My family! My wife! My children! I must rule the world! I must advance my position in life!" When a man has all these selfish ideas, how can he possibly create peace for others?

However, if he severs these qualities from himself and begins to feel the hunger, the pain, and the difficulties felt by others, and if he treats all lives as his own life, then he will find peace. If he can strive for this understanding and obtain inner patience, contentment, and trust in God,[1] if he can imbibe God's qualities and acquire God's state, then he will know peace. And once he finds that clarity within himself, he will discover peace in every life. If everyone would do this, life in this world would be heaven on earth. But if those who live in this world and rule this world cannot find serenity within themselves, they will only end up destroying the world when they

---

1. *ṣabr, shukr,* and *tawakkul 'alā Allāh*

try to establish peace. We must think about this.

One who has not found peace within himself will forever be giving speeches about peace. This world is a pulpit upon which man preaches, and there is no end to this talk! For millions of years man has been speaking this way, but he has not come forward to first find peace within himself. There is no use in making speeches. Man must acquire the qualities of God and live in that state. Only then can he speak of peace, only then can he speak the speech of God and dispense the justice of God's kingdom.

The people who have come to rule the world should think about this. Every man should think about it. Peace can only be found in the heart. Good qualities, wisdom, and clarity must provide that explanation within each heart. Man will only know peace when he brings God's justice and His qualities into himself. Therefore, before we speak of peace, let us try to acquire God's words within ourselves. Let us find tranquility within ourselves. If we can do that, our speech will be fruitful. Then the whole world will be at peace.

Man must find peace, tranquility, happiness, unity, love, and every good quality within his own life, within his own innermost heart.[2] Only a person who does that can understand the difficulties, the pain, and the misery of others. A man of wisdom will know this, understand this, and rectify his own mistakes. Then he can help others.

We must all think about this. May God help us. Amen.

---

2. *qalb*

قُدْرَةٌ

Qudrah

The power of God's grace

We must use God's power to avert the dangers and disasters that threaten mankind. If we can live with compassion and justice, then the laws of truth will govern, unity will live on, patience will be eternal, and compassion will never fail. Mankind must think of this. All of us must join together and bring peace to the Holy City.

JERUSALEM

The following letter was written in February, 1980, and was sent to prominent leaders of the Middle East and the free world.

A Letter to the Leaders of the World
Who Still Have Faith in Their Hearts

In the name of God, Most Merciful, Most Compassionate.

May God grant His help to all our brothers and sisters who have faith. Amen.

Jerusalem is not just the name of a city. *Salām* means peace, but today Jerusalem has become a place of conflict. We all have to reflect upon this. We must examine our hearts and consciences and ask ourselves, "What purpose is served by fighting and conquering lands? Does any conqueror live forever? Does anyone live forever?" We must analyze what has happened in the past and find a way to bring peace to Jerusalem.

The first part of this letter is a history of the events that took place in Jerusalem in the past. Please read this carefully. We write it in the hope that if we learn from the past we will correct our mistakes. If we realize the futility of these continuing conflicts, we can release ourselves from the bitterness that binds us and see our rightful duty toward all mankind. The second part of the letter describes how we should act in the present. We trust that each of you will read this with clarity in your hearts and then strive to bring peace and tranquility to the Holy City and to the world.

Please forgive me if there are any faults in what is written here. We are not attempting to present a complete history of Jerusalem; we merely wish to illustrate the futility of the constant warfare and bloodshed that has plagued the Holy City. All of us must join together and bring peace to Jerusalem. May God give good qualities, peace, and wisdom to all who trust in Him. May God give these to each heart. Amen.

A CHRONOLOGICAL HISTORY OF JERUSALEM
(Compiled for this letter in 2003—Dates are approximate)

1900 B.C.	Abraham enters Jerusalem. Melchizedek, King of Salem, welcomes and blesses him.
1300-1240 B.C.	Moses leads the Israelites from Egypt; his followers, led by Joshua, arrive in Canaan. Joshua defeats the King of Jerusalem, who is the head of the alliance of cities, but the city remains Jebusite.
1000 B.C.	David wrests Jerusalem from the Jebusites and makes it the capital of his kingdom.
970 B.C.	Solomon succeeds David as King of Israel.
950 B.C.	Solomon's Temple is completed.
928 B.C.	Shishak of Egypt sacks the city.
721 B.C.	Tiglath-Pileser of Assyria conquers northern Israel, and tiny Judea is all that remains of the empire of David and Solomon.
701 B.C.	Sennacherib, King of Assyria, lays siege to Jerusalem but is repelled.
587-86 B.C.	Nebuchadnezzar of Babylon conquers Jerusalem, destroys Solomon's Temple, exiles the Jews to Babylon, and for all intents and purposes, Judea ceases to exist.
539 B.C.	Cyrus of Persia topples the Babylonian Empire. Jerusalem is freed, Nebuchadnezzar's victims are released, and the descendants of David are allowed to return to Jerusalem. Construction of the second temple is begun under Sheshbazzara, a descendant of the house of David and Governor of Judah, and is continued by his nephew, Zerubbabel.
515 B.C.	The rebuilt temple of Solomon is inaugurated.
445 B.C.	Nehemiah completes the fortification of Jerusalem.
332 B.C.	Alexander the Great of Macedon conquers the Persian Empire but leaves Jerusalem untouched.
312 B.C.	After a series of battles between Alexander's generals, Ptolemy wins control over Jerusalem and takes Jewish prisoners to Alexandria.

312-198 B.C.	Rule of Ptolemaic dynasty.
198 B.C.	Antiochus III drives the Egyptians from the city.
198-169 B.C.	The Seleucids rule Jerusalem. Antiochus IV marches on Jerusalem to impose conformity of worship. The Jews are forced to conform to the Greek world and to give up circumcision and their codes of cleanliness and diet. They are also forced to worship Zeus. The temple is pillaged. Antiochus IV erects a pagan altar and sacrifices pigs before the idol of Zeus. The Scroll of the Law is torn up and burned.
164 B.C.	The Maccabees rise in rebellion and drive the Seleucids from the city and temple. They cleanse, purify, and rededicate the temple.
63 B.C.	Pompey and his Roman legions conquer Jerusalem. They defile the temple and dedicate it to Imperial Rome.
40 B.C.	The Romans are driven out and the city is briefly ruled by Mattathias Antigonus, the Hasmonean King. The Romans reconquer the city.
39 B.C.	Herod is chosen by the Romans to be King of the Jews. (Herod's father was an Arab who had been forcibly converted to Judaism, and so he was readily adapted for Roman uses. Mark Antony made him a Roman citizen, and thus his son, Herod, learned Roman politics.)
20 B.C.	Construction begins on Herod's temple.
4 B.C.	Birth of Jesus. Death of Herod.
29 A.D.	Trial of Jesus and his departure from the world.
66 A.D.	Gessius Florus' troops loot the temple's treasury, slaughtering worshipers and rabbis. This touches off the revolt of the population of Jerusalem.
70 A.D.	Titus captures, sacks, and destroys the second temple. Thousands upon thousands are killed, and again Jerusalem falls into the hands of the Romans. (Six hundred and fifty-seven years after the Babylonians plundered and razed the first temple, the second fell and none has risen since.)

132 A.D.	The Jews, led by Bar Kokhba, drive out the Romans and again make Jerusalem the Jewish capital.
135 A.D.	The Roman Emperor Hadrian destroys Jerusalem and builds on its site a city with new walls called Aelia Capitolina, with a temple on Mount Moriah dedicated to Jupiter. Hadrian bans the Jews from Jerusalem, and all Jews who defy the ban are executed.
324 A.D.	Constantine of Byzantium conquers Jerusalem.
325 A.D.	Constantine the Great embraces the Christian faith, thereby inaugurating the first Christian rule over the city. He marches under the flag of Jesus, uniting the Eastern and Western Roman Empires. The city of Jerusalem is rededicated. His mother, Helena, makes a pilgrimage to Jerusalem and identifies the sites for the Church of the Holy Sepulchre and the Church of the Nativity.
336 A.D.	Constantine builds the Church of the Holy Sepulchre. (This was the rebirth of Jerusalem, both as a spiritual center and as an objective of religious pilgrimage.)
570 A.D.	Birth of Muhammad.
614 A.D.	The Sassanid Persians led by Khosrau II push south through Palestine to the Sinai and Egypt, conquering Jerusalem, butchering 60,000 Christians, selling 35,000 into slavery, and demolishing the Christian shrines.
629 A.D.	The Byzantine Emperor Heraclius returns to Jerusalem, massacres the Jews, expels the survivors, and restores the ruined city.
630 A.D.	Mecca surrenders to Muhammad, and during the next seven years, the empire of Heraclius begins to fall to the rising Arab nation.
632 A.D.	Death of Muhammad.
638 A.D.	'Umar Ibn al-Khaṭṭāb, the second Muslim caliph, captures Jerusalem and builds the first mosque on the site where Solomon had erected the first temple. 'Umar is deeply conscious of Jerusalem's universal

sacredness and, during his rule, there is justice and freedom of worship. As 'people of the book', Christians are exempt from payment of a poll tax.

687 A.D. 'Abd al-Mālik orders the erection of the Dome of the Rock (the oldest Muslim sanctuary still standing in Jerusalem) for the purpose of attracting pilgrims to the Holy City.

691 A.D. Dome of the Rock completed. Christians and Muslims coexist peacefully and their pilgrims share the Holy City.

1077 A.D. A fierce band of Turkish nomads called Seljuks swarm through Persia, Iraq, and Egypt, finally seizing Jerusalem. For over twenty years the Christians are prevented from worshiping in the Holy City.

1096 A.D. In retaliation, the first crusaders depart for the Holy Land. Their number is made up of Christians from England, France, and Germany. Over 100,000 foot soldiers pillage and battle their way across Asia, without order or discipline. Less than ten percent reach Jerusalem.

1098 A.D. By the time the crusaders reach the Holy City, the Egyptians of the Fatmids Empire have recaptured the city. Though the Fatmids had always given Christians the freedom of the city, in 1099, the crusaders, led by Godfrey de Bouillon, capture Jerusalem, butchering its defendants and inhabitants, men, women, and children alike, and defile the Mosque of al-Aqsa and the Dome of the Rock. De Bouillon becomes the Defender of the Holy Sepulchre.

1100-1118 A.D. Reign of Baldwin I, first ruler of the Crusader Kingdom of Jerusalem. Plaster is applied over Arabic inscriptions, and the Dome of the Rock is transformed into a Christian church. Muslims and Jews are forbidden to reside in Jerusalem.

1187 A.D. Saladin, Vizier of Egypt, is determined to restore the Dome of the Rock to Arab rule. Through daring political and military maneuvers, he becomes King of Egypt and Syria. Finally, he achieves his objectives and captures Jerusalem. He restores Muslim and Jewish inhabitation of the city.

1192 A.D. Saladin and Richard the Lion-Hearted sign a five-year truce, ending the Third Crusade and giving Christians the right to make pilgrimages to Jerusalem.

1193 A.D. Saladin dies.

1229 A.D. The two succeeding monarchs, Sultan al-Kamil and Frederick II of Germany, briefly revert the Holy City to Christian rule. Warfare again sweeps the city and Jerusalem is again recaptured by the Arabs. Jerusalem would not again be governed by Christians for nearly seven centuries.

1250 A.D. The Mamelukes rise against the Ayyubid caliphs in Cairo, seize power in Egypt, and turn Palestine into an Egyptian province, beginning a 267 year reign of Egyptians, during which 47 sovereigns briefly sit upon the blood-stained throne.

1260 A.D. The city is pillaged by the Tartars.

1267 A.D. The Mamelukes take control of Jerusalem and inaugurate a period of architectural beautification of Muslim Jerusalem. They also rebuild the walls of the city.

1400 A.D. The city is sacked by Genghis Khan's Mongols.

1453 A.D. Muhammad II, a sultan of the Ottoman Turks, successfully besieges the city of Constantinople.

1517 A.D. Salim I (Muhammad II's grandson) captures Jerusalem from the Mameluke army. According to the original writs of 'Umar, he gives the Christians jurisdiction over their holy shrines.

1537 A.D. Suleiman the Magnificent, successor of Salim, begins his campaign to rebuild, beautify, and fortify Jerusalem.

1816 A.D. A decree of the reigning sultan allows the Jews free entrance to Palestine. From this time on, the Jewish population increases rapidly.

1827 A.D. United States opens the first diplomatic mission in Jerusalem.

1839 A.D.	British Consulate is established in Jerusalem, extending protection to the Jews.
1847 A.D.	The Catholic Church is renewed in Jerusalem.
1854 A.D.	The Crimean War is fought by Turkey, England, France, and Russia—ostensibly to settle the question of jurisdiction over Jerusalem's holy sites.
1860 A.D.	The first Jewish suburbs are built outside the walls.
1896 A.D.	Theodore Herzl publishes *The Jewish State,* a pamphlet which details a plan for the establishment of an autonomous Jewish state in Palestine under the authority of the sultan.
1897 A.D.	First Zionist Congress in Basel. The creation of a homeland for Jews in Palestine is proclaimed as the goal of the Zionist movement. There is a tremendous upsurge of Jewish migration to the Holy Land.
1917 A.D.	The British enter Jerusalem. The Ottoman army surrenders to the British. The Balfour Declaration puts Great Britain on record as favoring "a national home for the Jewish people." This declaration is then supported by France, the United States, and Italy.
1919 A.D.	The awakening Arab nationalism is voiced, with the Syrian Congress declaring its opposition to further Zionist migration.
1929 A.D.	Savage attacks on Jews in Jerusalem, Hebron, and Safad rekindle religious antagonism. The ancient Jewish communities of Safad and Hebron are almost wiped out.
1937 A.D.	Publication of the Royal (Peel) Commission, recommending the partition of Palestine.
1939-1945 A.D.	World War II. Six million Jews are killed by the Germans. British government issues White Paper in 1939, limiting immigration of Jewish refugees.
1945 A.D.	Germany surrenders and 30,000 Jews are released from Nazi concentration camps.
1946 A.D.	Underground, illegal immigration to Israel of Jewish survivors of the German concentration camps commences.

1947 A.D. United Nations votes partition of Palestine and creates Israel as the new Jewish state.

1948 A.D. British withdraw from Palestine. The state of Israel is proclaimed with Jerusalem as its capital. War engulfs the area. Jerusalem is partitioned.

1951 A.D. King ʽAbdullah of Transjordan, early advocate of Arab confederation, assassinated in the Mosque al-Aqsa.

1956 A.D. War. The Sinai Campaign.

1967 A.D. Six-day War: Israelis seize Golan Heights, Sinai, Gaza, the West Bank, and Old Jerusalem from the Arab Nations. The city is under Israeli rule.

1973 A.D. Yom Kippur War.

1977 A.D. President Anwar Sadat of Egypt visits Jerusalem, opening the prospect for peace.

1979 A.D. Israel and Egypt sign a peace treaty at Camp David. A timetable is set for returning captured lands. The process of returning the lands and normalization of relationship is begun.

1980 A.D. Jerusalem Basic Law enacted declaring united Jerusalem to be capital of Israel.

1981 A.D. President Anwar Sadat of Egypt assassinated.

1994 A.D. Mutual recognition of Israel and the Palestinian Authority.

Warren Christopher, the United States Secretary of State, visits Chairman Yasir Arafat and the Palestinian National Council—the first of more than a dozen trips by United States Secretaries of State.

Jordan and Israel sign a peace treaty calling for close economic and political cooperation.

1995 A.D. Israeli Prime Minister Yitzhak Rabin assassinated by an ultra-nationalist Israeli opposed to Rabin's Land-for-Peace agreements with the Palestinians.

1998 A.D. President Bill Clinton persuades Israeli Prime Minister Netanyahu to allow United States involvement in security negotiations.

President Clinton addresses Palestinian Authority.

1999 A.D. Talks between Israeli Prime Minister Ehud Barak and Syrian Foreign Minister Farouk al-Sharaa begin in Washington D.C.

2000 A.D. President Clinton convenes intensive peace talks at Camp David between Israel and the Palestinians. Talks collapse.

Ariel Sharon, prior to his election as Prime Minister of Israel, visits one of the holiest sites in Jerusalem, the Temple Mount, also known as Haram al-Sharif. A second Palestinian *intifada* quickly follows.

2001 A.D. Intense peace talks between Egypt and Israel end without an agreement.

International commission headed by former United States Senator George Mitchell submits a report calling for an end to the violence. Both sides accept the report but with different interpretations.

United States CIA Director George Tenet works with both sides to implement the Mitchell plan, but the effort stalls.

2002 A.D. United States Secretary of State Colin Powell concludes a ten-day trip to the Middle East without securing a cease-fire between the Palestinian Authority and the Israelis.

The Arab League makes a proposal which would establish peace in the region.

(This chronological history was compiled by the Publisher of the Fellowship Press.)

Within the story of Jerusalem is the history of the entire world. From the time of Adam until now there has been constant fighting. Wars have occurred all over the world for these two hundred million years, but they have been especially concentrated in this central point of Jerusalem ever since the time of Abraham. We have witnessed so many blood baths in this area; we have seen the cutting off of heads and hands and so many other acts of cruelty and violence. Every person of every religion who has heard of this sacrifice of human life and these rivers of blood must realize what is happening. We who belong to the human race must learn from the example of Jerusalem, for the history of this Holy City shows us the state of the world.

Jerusalem should be a sacred shrine, a place where the entire human race can worship God in peace. If human beings of all four religions would only understand this and live in unity, then this place of worship would not be a battlefield. If people of all races and nationalities ever hope to live as one human race, they must have absolute faith in the one God. That is mankind's only treasure.

To witness that there is one God and to establish His word and His compassion in the hearts of the people, God sent many prophets to the world. He sent 124,000 in all. Twenty-five of them are mentioned in the Qur'an, and their stories are also recounted in the Bible and Torah. From the time of Adam, they came here to develop unity and faith in God, so that the human race would live in peace and tolerance as one family, accepting one God, the Day of Judgment, and the justice of God's laws.

If the human race had realized the meaning of God's message, they would not have indulged in the frenzy of wars which have resulted in bloodshed and the destruction of lives. But instead, in every country where the prophets delivered their message, the people became divided among themselves. Some believed in religion but not in God; some clung to racial differences but not to God. However, there were some who did have faith in God. A few accepted God and all the prophets and even believed that all people were the children of Adam.

The majority, however, only sought titles and positions. They were ready to conquer lands for the sake of gold, property, and worldly possessions, but they would not accept the words of God or nurture His compassionate qualities. They refused to accept the kingdom of love which encompasses mercy, tolerance, and equality. Instead they ruled their kingdoms with selfishness, preferring to worship satan, animals, snakes, scorpions, and spirits, and trusting in the miracles of demons, earth, fire, water, air, the sun and the moon, and illusion. Those rulers believed in the power of such miracles and used them to try to destroy God and to undermine faith in Him and in truth, equality, and peace.

It does not matter whether those rulers conquered Jerusalem or Egypt or the entire world, for they are no longer here. Even the land itself has changed. Part of it has been lost to the sea, and some places which the sea once covered have again become land. Where forests once stood, cities have arisen, and ancient cities are now buried under forests. Cemeteries have become cities, and cities have turned into cemeteries. Over the centuries, many parts of the world have been destroyed by the sea, by wind, by rain, by fire, and by earthquakes.

We have related the history of Jerusalem to show that whoever rules there now will ultimately move on, just as all those who ruled there throughout the ages have moved on. They are no longer alive. This is the truth. Therefore, in this one place which all four religions honor, let us come together as one and establish what is unchanging. Let us worship the one Almighty God. He is the very form of compassion. He may be called by any name in any language: God, Andavan, Rahman, Adonai, Allah, or Yahweh, but He is still the One God. All the religions of the human race must realize this. May each of us understand and cut from our hearts any thoughts of divisiveness.

My brothers and sisters, we must think about the state of the world today. We must reflect on the fate of Jerusalem. The age of destruction has now dawned, and we are approaching a third world war. Groups have emerged which represent the Antichrist.[1] Wherever faith in God still exists, those who deny His existence are creeping in, trying to divide lands, disrupt the peace of the people, and create poverty—all under the false promise of peace and stability. They join hands with those who have lost their faith in God and turned to the world because of poverty or some other sorrow in their lives. They seek out areas where despair exists, destroy everything there that is good, foster all that is evil, tear bodies apart, and bring torment to all lives. They indulge in selfish acts and cause untold suffering.

Ever since such people first emerged, they have infiltrated different lands, spreading their false propaganda, destroying faith in God, and eventually becoming dictators. They rule by force and soak the

1. Dajjāl

earth with blood. Such is the state of the world in this century.

All the countries with faith in God must unite! Those who have conscience, those who have justice and wisdom and compassion in their hearts must unite to carry out the laws of justice and bring peace and equality to the people of the world. We must search out hardship wherever it exists and attempt to alleviate the suffering that accompanies it. We must discover the areas which have already been infiltrated by those agents without faith in God, agents whom many countries are now willing to follow. If the leading figures in the United Nations and the governments of all the larger nations will join together to seek out the places where this poison has penetrated, we can remove the needle through which it was injected and show the countries of the world a path whereby they can find some peace and live in unity. Then these poisonous germs will lose their ability to infect new areas and their power to destroy what is good.

Peace will then flourish and justice will prevail, as it did before. Honesty and integrity will rise again, and the people of the world will live in a state of lasting peace.

England, France, Israel, the United States, the Arab nations, Canada, Australia, and all the other countries which still have faith in God must reflect upon this. World peace, unity, compassion, and goodness are in danger of being lost. If we look at what has happened in Jerusalem, we will realize how urgent and necessary it is to take action.

It is true that the United States, England, and other countries have at one time or other engaged in wars, but they have always shown compassion and returned the conquered countries to independent rule, allowing them to live in freedom. They have helped to avert other wars which would have come to those lands, and they have protected them in times of danger. The British Empire grew far and wide, once extending from sunrise to sunset, but now England has returned to her own shores, and those colonies have been returned to their own people. However, the evil germ that has crept in among some of those countries today is creating endless trouble. This faction disrupts the unity of the world for its own gain, forever seeking to expand its dominion even further. Ruling by the gun, it forces people to do as they are told, without protest. It imposes its own values and its own government upon other countries, denying them any freedom.

If we think about this, we will recognize the difference between a power that wants to return freedom to a conquered people and a power that refuses to release the people. We who have faith in God must see how different these two approaches are.

It was to release us from the tyranny of those who lack faith in God and deny His existence that every one of the prophets came. They came to release us from the grip of poverty and the slavery of the soul. They came to release us from satan, from illusion, from the bondage of our bodies, and from the bondage of governments. They released us from all these forces that enslaved us and gave us a place to live in unity and freedom, did they not?

When the colonists first came to America more than two hundred years ago, they encountered great hardship. Thinking back on its own history, the United States must be aware of the plight of other countries and realize that this same hardship may come to them again one day. We are not different from other people. Understanding the suffering of others, we all must act with compassion and love and avoid causing any more suffering to anyone. We must follow what our conscience tells us is good and strive to allow everyone to live in freedom and peace.

Living together in unity as brothers and sisters is a sign of the children who accept God and who will rule His kingdom. The people of Israel, Egypt, the Arab nations, the United States, and all countries must reflect deeply on this.

There is one other area upon which the larger nations need to focus their attention. On the day that an amicable settlement is achieved between the Palestinians and Israel, divisiveness will be erased, wars will stop, peace will be assured, and the destruction will be halted. The only hope for that area lies in convincing these two groups to live in unity as peaceful neighbors, with border security maintained between the two lands by a United Nations Peace Force.

Look at Jerusalem. How many wars have been fought, how many people have ruled, how many have been enslaved, how much danger and suffering there has been! If we can understand this and bring peace to Jerusalem, then all those who believe in God can live in unity. Lack of faith in God is the root of all enmity. And that divisiveness will cease only if those who reject God can be kept from infiltrating Jerusalem. On the very day that this is realized by all people who believe in God, no matter what religion they might follow, religious differences will disappear and the battles will stop. There will be no more murders, no more blood baths. All differences will be cut away.

Each one of you, the United Nations, America, Europe, the African and Arab countries, Israel, England, and all others who trust in God must realize this basic cause of enmity and cut it away. I say this because the war of destruction seems to be imminent, and I can see where the enemy is. All must join in unity, now!

God accepts Jews, Christians, and Muslims alike. All are found in Jerusalem, yet those who have faith in God as well as those who do not have faith in God continue to fight over that land, even though it only results in destruction. There have been many who have ruled that area and many who have even ruled the earth, but they are all gone. And there are still more to come who will rule and then pass on. No one can rule forever.

Please reflect on this and realize that other than God all else will change. Everything in this world changes; only God remains the same forever. If mankind will realize this truth, then we can avert disaster by coming together with faith in God and living in unity and compassion. Do not live divided. With compassion for each other, live in unity and truth, in the presence of God. Live according to justice and conscience, respecting the lives and bodies of all others as your own, and knowing the hunger and the suffering of others as your own. Have patience, contentment, trust in God, and live praising God at all times,[2] and peace will be easy.

It is not customary for me to speak about politics. But when I look at what is happening now, I see the world threatened by the dangers of atomic energies and the arrogance of human beings. I see how much suffering is being caused by the obstinancy and selfish-

2. *ṣabr, shukr, tawakkul 'alá Allāh,* and *al-ḥamdu lillāh*

ness of mankind. And I see that it will end in destruction.

This state is fast approaching, and all of us will die. We must realize this and take the proper steps to avert disaster before the bombs start falling. Very soon those bombs might burst in our hands. But if we can establish a state of peace, we might gain victory over destruction.

All these things have happened before, and they are happening again. And to what avail? We must learn to live as one human race, worship one God, and fashion laws of righteousness and justice which will take us back to our Creator. That will provide exaltedness to our lives. That will elevate our lives.

We must all attain this state. This is why I most humbly ask all of you to try to avert the disaster that threatens us. Let there be unity among mankind. If we live without the differences of I and you, we can escape from this imminent destruction. Instead of trying to cure the illness of our differences with the arrogance that thinks, "We are better than they are!" we must cure that illness by using God's tolerance and His other gracious qualities. We must use God's power to avert the dangers and disasters that threaten mankind. If we can live with compassion and justice, then laws of truth will govern, unity will live on, patience will be eternal, and compassion will never fail. Absolute justice will reign forever. Mankind must think of this.

All of us must join together to bring peace to the Holy City.

May God give His grace, the wealth of the three worlds, undiminishing life, and peace without sorrow to my loving brothers and sisters, to those who are older than I, to those who are younger than I, and to all who have been born with me. Amen.

I am writing this letter to show how peace could be brought to the world. If we who are the human generation can bring such peace to fruition, then we can reach exaltedness in our lives. Everyone with wisdom and faith must realize this. I am speaking out of the awareness which comes from my heart. This is not being said to attack anyone, to find fault with anyone, or to show differences toward anyone. If there are any faults in what I have said, please forgive me. If there are mistakes in this letter, I am asking everyone who reads it to please forgive me. Amen.

Allah is sufficient unto all. Amen.

Mu'min

A true believer

If we are true believers, we will not see any differences between others and ourselves. We will see only One. We will see Allah, one human race, and one justice for all. That justice and truth is the strength of Islam.

JUSTICE FOR ALL

اَعُوذُ بِاللهِ مِنَ الشَّيْطَانِ الرَّجِيمِ بِسْمِ اللهِ الرَّحْمٰنِ الرَّحِيمِ

I seek refuge in Allah from the evils of the accursed satan.
In the name of Allah, Most Merciful, Most Compassionate.

There is a traditional story[1] about 'Umar Ibn al-Khaṭṭāb, the Islamic caliph who captured the city of Jerusalem and built the first mosque on the grounds of the sacred sanctuary now known as the Dome of the Rock.[2]

'Umar was a ruler of great justice and peace. Because of his noble qualities, he was given the beautiful name, Commander of the Faithful,[3] and it was his rightful duty to receive the key to the Holy City which was the original *qiblah,* the direction Muslims face while praying.

The armies of 'Umar had already entered Jerusalem and taken control of the city from the Christians who had ruled there since the time of Constantine, but when 'Umar came to take official possession of Jerusalem, he came alone. He journeyed from Damascus to Jerusalem with only one camel and a cameleer. The caliph, being a man of great humility, had arranged with the cameleer that they would both take turns riding the camel. According to justice, he would ride for a while, then the cameleer would ride and he would walk.

Meanwhile, the entire city was awaiting 'Umar's impending arrival. The bishop of the Holy Sepulcher had announced, "The great Islamic leader is coming! We must greet him and pay our

1. *ḥadīth*

2. *al-Bayt al-Muqaddas*

3. *Amīr al-Mu'minīn*

respects to him." And so all the people had gathered at the city gate, awaiting a grand royal procession. But no procession appeared.

Instead, two people became visible on the horizon, approaching very slowly. When they finally reached the city, it was the cameleer's turn to be riding, and so all the people mistook him for the caliph and rushed to greet him.

"Wait! I am not the caliph!" he protested and explained their arrangement to take turns riding and walking. The people, overwhelmed by this justice, praised the great caliph.

The bishop was also amazed by such justice. His heart filled with joy, and he handed the key of the city to 'Umar Ibn al-Khaṭṭāb.

The bishop then invited 'Umar to perform his prayers within their church. But when 'Umar saw the interior decorated with all the Christian symbols, he politely declined, saying, "I will pray just outside your doors."

Once he had finished, the bishop asked, "Why would you not come inside our church?"

"If I had prayed in your sanctuary," 'Umar explained, "my followers and those who come here in the future would take over this building and turn it into a mosque. They would destroy your place of worship. To avoid these difficulties and allow your church to continue as it is, I prayed outside."

Again the bishop was amazed by his justice. "Today, because of your justice, faith, wisdom, and truth, you have received the key to the Holy City. But for how long will this remain in your hands? When will this sacred place come back into our possession?"

'Umar Ibn al-Khaṭṭāb then replied, "Today we have indeed taken over this place of worship. It is with the four qualities of faith, wisdom, justice, and truth that we have regained the city. As long as these four exist in Islam, as long as the Muslims have all four in their hands, they will retain the city. But when these qualities depart from Islam, this place of worship will change hands once again.

"If it happens that we must lose this place to someone else, it will be because we lack certitude in our faith. When the Muslims sell the truth and collect worldly wealth and seek worldly pleasures;

when they lose good faith, good conduct, and the good behavior of modesty and reserve; when they relate to women in an immoral and unjust way; when they behave with backbiting, jealousy, and envy; when they lack unity and establish hypocrisy; when they destroy good deeds and degenerate into committing evil actions—when all this occurs in the midst of Islam, then unity and peacefulness will be destroyed. These evil qualities and actions will cause divisions and separations, and this Holy City will be taken from our hands. That is certain.

"When this happens, the followers of Islam will be as numerous as the granules of flour in dough. But the number of those who shall take possession of the city will be as few as the grains of salt in the dough. This will happen when degradation permeates Islam."

These were the words of 'Umar Ibn al-Khaṭṭāb when he took possession of the Holy City and the sacred ground of the Dome of the Rock.

My brethren, we have to understand the state of Islam today and reflect upon the words of 'Umar Ibn al-Khaṭṭāb. When he was given the key to the Holy City, he spoke about four essential things which must always exist in Islam: justice, truth, wisdom, and faith. As long as Islam retains these four and lives in unity, comforting with compassion and giving peace to other lives, there will be peace in Islam. But when this justice changes, peace will be lacking. The time is now approaching when we will find no peace in Islam or in the hearts of the people. We must realize that if man wants peace and justice in the world and in his life, then he himself must conduct his life with good qualities. That is the only way man will find peace anywhere. Islam and the human society must realize this.

Each one of us should reflect and understand what we must do. We must develop and strengthen our faith, certitude, and determination. Each person must look within, find clarity, and raise that benevolent flag of Islam in his life.

Before the time of the Prophet Muhammad, the Arab nations underwent tremendous difficulties. There was so much poverty, famine, and sorrow. Then through the Prophet's pleading for God's blessings, these countries received the amazing wealth of faith.[4] The light of Islam burned in every house. The undiminishing wealth of patience, contentment, trust in God, and praise of God[5] filled every heart. Because of the Prophet's prayers and because of the richness of faith, certitude, and determination, Almighty God changed the desert into His benevolence. Where there was not even water to drink, He made oil, and that oil was converted into gold and jewels. Endless wealth was poured into the desert where nothing would grow and was given to the community of Islam, and that wealth still exists there today. Almighty God gave them this because of their faith, did He not? But if the community of Islam now forfeits that treasure of faith, then those earthly treasures will be lost. You and I should realize this.

In another traditional story, the Prophet said, "Do not waste your fortune, do not waste your money, do not throw away your wealth, do not waste anything. Instead, share it with your brothers. Help your brothers, take care of them, and take care of your relatives. Do not be wasteful." We who are *Īmān-Islām*[6] must understand this today. If all the leaders, the teachers, the sheikhs, and the respected ones understood this, no one would be poor in Islam.

Allah has said that kings and beggars must pray to Him side by side, embrace each other heart to heart and give greetings of peace[7] at each time of prayer. He has given us this way to express the unity of Islam to everyone who is accepted by the Qur'an. And since nothing can be found in the words of the Qur'an that indicates showing any differences among people, everyone in the world must be accepted.

The Qur'an speaks of twenty-five prophets, which include Adam, Noah, Abraham, Ishmael, Moses, David, Jesus, Muhammad,

---

4. *īmān*

5. *ṣabr, shukr, tawakkul 'alá Allāh,* and *al-ḥamdu lillāh*

6. *Īmān:* absolute faith, certitude, and determination.
Islām: the state of absolute purity. See glossary.

7. *salāms*

Idris, Isaac, Job, Salih, Joseph, and Jonah, may the peace of Allah be upon them all. The prophets, the saints, the angels, and the great holy men of divine wisdom[8] are all spoken of in the traditional stories and in other holy books:

There is no god other than Allah, and Adam is the pure one of Allah.
Lā ilāh illā Allāh Adam Safī Allāh.

There is no god other than Allah, and Noah is the one saved by Allah.
Lā ilāh illā Allāh Nūh Najī Allāh.

There is no god other than Allah, and Abraham is the friend of Allah.
Lā ilāh illā Allāh Ibrāhīm Khalīl Allāh.

There is no god other than Allah, and Ishmael is the sacrifice of Allah.
Lā ilāh illā Allāh Ismā 'īl Dhabīḥ Allāh.

There is no god other than Allah, and Moses is the one who spoke with Allah.
Lā ilāh illā Allāh Mūsá Kalīm Allāh.

There is no god other than Allah, and David is the prince of His faithful.
Lā ilāh illā Allāh Dāwūd Khalīfat Allāh.

There is no god other than Allah, and Jesus is the soul of Allah.
Lā ilāh illā Allāh 'Īsa Rūḥ Allāh.

There is no god other than Allah, and Muhammad is His Messenger,
may Allah bless him and grant him peace.
Lā ilāh illā Allāh Muḥammad Rasūl Allāh ṣallá Allāh 'alayhi wa-sallam.

Allah sent down each of the prophets and directed them to preach His commandments. Their message came from His resonance. He alone sent them the revelations[9] and gave them the words. Therefore, we must not see the prophets as differing from each other; they should only be seen as one. Allah does not reject any of them.

The Qur'an does not show hatred toward any religion; it accepts them all as paths leading to the One. Can we then reject any of these

8. *quṭbs*

9. *waḥy*

teachings, considering them separate from ourselves? No, we must take everything embraced by the Qur'an into our hearts. We are told in the Qur'an to accept what is accepted by God and to discard what is discarded by God. Satan, alcohol, drugs, falsehood, jealousy, anger, sins, the arrogance of the I, and other evil qualities and actions like these are discarded by the Qur'an. They are all opposed by the Qur'an, by Allah, and by the messengers of God,[10] and therefore should also be discarded by the heart of a true human being. That heart is the true Qur'an and should be a place where only faith and love for Allah dwell. True man[11] should accept only Allah's duties, Allah's commands, and the resonance of the Qur'an. That is justice and that is Islam.

But think about what we are doing now! If we understood and accepted the words of Prophet Muhammad and the words of the Qur'an, we would not consider anyone our enemy; we would not fight with anyone. We would not see any differences or cause any opposition. Everyone who accepted God would be a brother to us. This is what the Qur'an points out. No matter what religion or scripture or prophet people may follow, all are the children of Adam, all belong to the family of Abraham. They are our brothers and followers of Muhammad. There is one sun and one moon. They do not show any differences toward the things they shine upon. When the rain falls does it fall on one thing and not another? When the wind blows does it show any differences? No, it blows the same way for all. Does the earth show preferences? Does water show any differences?

In the same way, Islam must not see any differences between one life and another. Like the sun and the moon, Islam should perform its duty and show its love to everyone alike. The sun showers its brilliant rays upon the whole world, and the moon gives its cooling light, dispelling the darkness. In the same way, Islam should dispel the dark torpor of evil. It should give cooling love to all hearts.

Allah gave man this benevolent umbrella of Islam, the umbrella

10. *rasūls*

11. *insān*

of His grace. To have equality, justice, compassion, unity, tranquility, and peace—this is Islam. Divisiveness is not Islam. Truth, compassion, and unity are Islam. Tranquility and peace are Islam. To end the worries of all lives and to embrace all lives is Islam. This is the message of the Qur'an, the treasure that came from the resonance of Allah. Islam should understand this. These were the instructions, the truths, and the justice given to the prophets.

O brothers and sisters, think about this. This same truth can be found in the traditional stories, which we have already spoken about. We can understand many things from them. On the outside, they are stories, but when we examine them with wisdom and with faith and certitude, we can see the real meaning inside. Just as there is a difference between the inside and outside of a mirror, a difference exists in everything that the eyes can see. A snake looks beautiful on the outside, but it is full of poison inside. Some fruits that look beautiful on the outside may have no taste, while others that look ugly may be very tasty. Such differences also exist in the divine knowledge[12] that we learn, in the wisdom that we learn, in the qualities and actions that we learn, and in the body. Differences exist between the outside and the inside of everything. Therefore, we must look at both in order to understand the meaning.

However, true Islam is the same on the inside and the outside. Its actions are the same inside and out. Its justice and its words are the same. We must understand this. Allah is the only One who is not hidden by any outer covering. Neither is Islam hidden by anything. A light which has nothing blocking it is pure light. The word that contains no envy is a true word. That which shows no differences is love. True unity does not distinguish between high and low. True compassion considers all lives as its own and does duty without showing preferences. True justice is to act without the difference of 'mine' and 'yours'. Conscience is to realize one's own faults rather than looking at the faults of others. It is to understand the state of another and say, "If I were in his place, wouldn't I have done this also? If I had been in his state of poverty, I too might have stolen and

---

12. *'ilm*

lied the way he did. Therefore I share in his guilt." Having understood this, we must show patience and contentment. We must realize why that man acted as he did, then comfort him, give him love, help him to be peaceful, and bring him to the good path. That is Islam. That is what is called conscience.

Like this, in every way we have to look at our own faults and understand the faults of others. Then we must correct our faults and give peace to the others. If we are true believers,[13] we will not see any differences between others and ourselves. We will see only One. We will see Allah, one human race, and one justice for all. That justice and truth is the strength of Islam. That compassion and peace is the strength of Islam. That unity gives strength and peace to man in this life and in the hereafter.[14] That is *Īmān-Islām.* Islam is Allah's good gift. It is the completeness and resplendence that gives peace to all lives. It is love, grace, unity, and compassion. It is to live as one race and one family. That is Islam.

It is this that conquers the world by conquering every heart with love. It is compassion that conquers. It is unity that conquers. It is Allah's good qualities, behavior, and actions that conquer others. It is this state that is called Islam. The sword doesn't conquer; love is sharper than the sword. Love is an exalted, gentle sword.

My brethren, peacefulness and equality are greater than anger. Instead of gaining victory by fighting, use the sword of patience. That is the best way to receive Allah's wealth. Try to understand the outside and know the inside. Then you will receive that good gift of *Īmān-Islām.* As long as this state does not develop within us it is certain that destruction will occur. The life of man and the world will both be destroyed.

However, if we conduct ourselves with the qualities of Allah, then Islam will never be in a low state and truth will never decline. Goodness will not decline. The kingdom of heaven and the kingdom of Allah's truth and justice will always be in His hand. As long as we hold onto good qualities and actions, this world will be the hereafter,

---

13. *mu'min*

14. *ākhirah*

and our life here will be a life in heaven, a life of grace. That is certain. This is true Islam. These are Allah's words, given in His commandments and in the revelations that were sent down to the Prophet. May we in Islam think about this.

This is the certitude of the heart of Bawa Muhaiyaddeen. Forgive me if there are any mistakes or faults.

May all the peace, the beneficence, and the blessings of God be upon you.[15] Amen.

---

15. *al-salām 'alaykum wa-raḥmat Allāh wa-barakātuhu kulluh*

دَوْلَةٌ

Dawlah

The wealth of God

God's wealth is all you need for your life and for the resplendence of your soul. Even if you rule the world, obtain titles and status, and acquire great treasures and land, you will never find peace. The only peace you can find is in God, in His qualities, His actions, His justice, His compassion, His patience, and His unity.

PEACE CAN ONLY BE FOUND IN GOD

أَعُوذُ بِٱللَّهِ مِنَ ٱلشَّيْطَٰنِ ٱلرَّجِيمِ بِسْمِ ٱللَّهِ ٱلرَّحْمَٰنِ ٱلرَّحِيمِ

I seek refuge in Allah from the evils of the accursed satan.
In the name of Allah, Most Merciful, Most Compassionate.

May all the peace, the beneficence, and the blessings of God be upon you.[1]

For those of us who have faith in God alone, there is only one teaching. Whatever religion we belong to, whether it be Hinduism, Zoroastrianism, Christianity, Judaism, or Islam, and whatever prayers we say, what is it that we are really searching for? Only one thing—that treasure which is God. But those who have no faith need many things in this world. They find satisfaction in unjust actions, political disturbances, jealousy, deceit, selfishness, and pride. Those who search for these things will never find peace or equality. They lead a life without unity, justice, or peace. That is their hell, and they make this endless hell their life.

However, any society that recognizes the one God and holds nothing equal to Him, any society that holds onto that one Truth, worshiping one Master, praying to Him, and surrendering to Him—any society that has reached that state of understanding needs only God. The people of such a society need only God's qualities, His actions, His conduct, His grace, His patience, and His compassion. What else is there that matters?

All who have faith in God are striving and searching for the same thing. Therefore, we must have no divisions of race, religion, or caste, for wherever there are separations we can never see God. Only in the place where no divisions exist can one see God. These

1. *al-salām 'alaykum wa-raḥmat Allāh wa-barakātuhu kulluh*

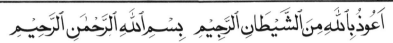

divisions keep us apart from His qualities, from His grace, from His treasure, from His justice, from His knowledge, and from His truth and peace. They separate us from God. Those who have such differences within will never find peace.

We must realize that the human society is one. We are all the children of Adam, and there is only one God and one prayer. The Bible, the Hindu Puranas, the Zend-Avesta, the Torah, and the Qur'an—all these scriptures contain the words of grace given by God to the prophets. That grace is light. If you look at these scriptures on the outside you will see only a book, nothing more. If you look inside the cover, you will find pages, letters, words, sentences, and stories. But if you look deep within, you will find Allah, the words of Allah, the duties of the prophets, the commandments, the power, and the light.

Allah placed all these explanations inside man and told him to look at them with understanding. This vast treasure contains His three thousand gracious qualities, His ninety-nine actions,[2] His justice and peacefulness, heaven, hell, and the entire world. Allah made all this into the innermost heart[3] of man and within that heart He placed a light. Then, to explain the light inside, He gave the scriptures on the outside. God told man, "Your body is a book and your heart is a heaven. Your wisdom is a resplendent light, and I am the power within that wisdom. The innermost heart of man is My kingdom, the kingdom which I rule. This is My history and your history. When you understand this, you will live in unity. You will be My slave[4] and I will be your Master. Then I can give you whatever you need and make you peaceful."

Therefore, when you study the Qur'an and other scriptures, you must take the inner meaning, place it deep inside, and look at it with understanding. Then speak the words of God with God, who is your wisdom. Speak God's truth with God, who is truth itself. Demonstrate the qualities of God, who is those qualities. Practice God's actions every day of your life. Be within the justice of God and

---

2. *wilāyāt*

3. *qalb*

4. *'abd*

do what is just. Be within the compassionate eyes of God and then look at the world. Be in the state of God's peacefulness and try to give peace to the world. Be in the state of God's unity and then try to establish unity in the world.

When you exist in the state of God's actions and conduct and then speak with Him, that power will speak with you. If you do not reach that state, then the words you speak will not be the truth. If you just keep the Bible or other scriptures on the outside, those scriptures will be only books full of words. And that is all you will understand. But if you become a representative of God and speak with that power, then that power will speak with you. If you become a true man[5] and a representative of God, then God will become your Master and you will understand the words which are His divine knowledge.[6]

Until the day you find this state within yourself, you will only be studying the separations and differences that exist between races and religions. None of the lessons you learn in this world from books or scriptures, from poetry or other writings, will ever bring you peace. You will never understand the meaning within them; you will only see the cover, the pages, and the letters. God's words are alive, shining as the resplendence within. If you cannot see that, you will never understand.

We must know our story, God's story. We must know His power, His vibration, His truth and peacefulness. Separations and differences are the faults within us that destroy our unity and peace. If we understand this, we will find peace in God's kingdom, in life, and in the family of mankind. Then we can truly understand the scriptures of Hinduism, Zoroastrianism, Christianity, Judaism, and Islam. They all contain the truth. But desire and the monkey mind have no truth, and when we look through those eyes, with the thoughts of 'our book' and 'our sect', we see only differences. When we are under the influence of this chloroform, this alcohol, our wisdom is clouded and we see only differences. But when we free ourselves from such torpor and acquire God's qualities, wisdom,

---

5. *insān*

6. *'ilm*

and actions, when we speak in that state as the representatives of God, then we will know the worth of the Qur'an, the Bible, and all the scriptures. Only then will we know the value of God and the value of man. How can we ever understand without achieving this state? Let us think about this.

When you dig a well, you must dig deep down until you reach a spring. Can the well ever be filled without reaching that deep source? If you depend upon the rain or some other outer source to fill the well, the water will simply evaporate or be absorbed by the earth. Then how can you wash yourself or quench your thirst? Only if you reach deep enough to find a spring will you come upon an undiminishing source of water. Similarly, if you merely read the words of the scriptures, without digging deeper for their meaning, it is like digging a well without ever reaching the spring or like trying to fill it with rainwater. Neither will be sufficient. Only when you open that spring within and divine knowledge flows from it will the water of God's qualities fill your heart. Only then can you receive His wealth. Only then will you find peace and tranquility. This wisdom and divine knowledge must arise from within you; the story of God and prayer must be understood from within. Then you will have all the water you need for yourself, and you will also have enough to share with others.

When a prospector searches for gold, he must sift the earth in order to extract this precious metal. He takes what is valuable and discards the rest. Similarly, wherever you search, whether it be in the east, west, north, or south, whether it be in Hinduism, Zoroastrianism, Christianity, Judaism, or Islam, you must search for and extract only that one valuable thing, the gold, the treasure of God, the truth. As you search through all the scriptures, you must discard everything else, just as the prospectors discard the dirt and stones. God's wealth[7] is all you need for your life and for the resplendence of your soul.

Until you understand this, you will know nothing but disturbances in your life. Even if you rule the world, obtain titles and status, and acquire great treasures and land, you will never find

---

7. *dawlah*

peace. The only peace you can find is in God, in His qualities, His actions, His justice, His compassion, His patience, and His unity. Remember this.

Once you thought that everything you studied and learned was the truth. But then you progressed to the next step, and found that all you had learned was not the truth. And in the future when you go still one step further and look back upon all that you presently hold to be true, you will see that it, too, is false. In this way, each time you advance to a new level, you will find that all you learned in the past was false. Finally, when you reach the state of God and the state of His wisdom, you will realize that all your thoughts were false. Everything was false. Only He is truth. His wisdom is the real truth, and His qualities are the real gold.

When you understand this, you will ask His forgiveness for all the faults that you committed in the past. You will see clearly and absolutely that there is only one family, one prayer, and one God. You must think about this. This is the valuable wisdom, the wisdom of truth.

Therefore, find unity within yourself. Find peace within yourself. Find equality within yourself. Only when that spring opens within you and flows forth can you feed others and give them peace.

Children of wisdom, you must have love for God alone and faith in God alone. If you strengthen your faith, certitude, and determination,[8] and open the spring of God's wisdom, then all the suffering of this birth, this mind, and this world will be washed away. All the opposition you face in this life, all the pain and suffering you may undergo at the time of death, and all the suffering you may have to face on Judgment Day will be cleansed by that water of God's grace. It will bring you to a state of death before death and make you a pure, resplendent light form. That faith will wash away the karma of your birth and transform you into a pure resplendence which no dirt can touch. You will become the resplendence within the resplendence which is God. You will know the value and the beauty of God. You will shine as one who has destroyed the karma in all three worlds, and you will have freedom

---

8. *īmān*

in all three worlds. You will realize that you came from Him, that you have grown within Him and become pure, and that He has accepted you. He will be a mystical resplendence, and you will be a light form.

You must become one. Only if you pray to God with faith will peace and unity come to your life. And only then can you give peace to the world. Think about this. Amen.

PART TWO:
HOLY WAR

جِهَادٌ

Jihād

Holy war

For man to raise his sword against man, for man to kill man, is not holy war. True holy war is to praise God and to cut away the enemies of truth within our own hearts. We must cast out all that is evil within us, all that opposes God. This is the war that we must fight.

THE HOLY WAR WITHIN

أَعُوذُ بِاللّٰهِ مِنَ الشَّيْطَانِ الرَّجِيمِ بِسْمِ اللّٰهِ الرَّحْمٰنِ الرَّحِيمِ

I seek refuge in Allah from the evils of the accursed satan.
In the name of Allah, Most Merciful, Most Compassionate.

God is Most Great. God is Most Great. *Allāh Akbar. Allāh Akbar.* There is no god other than God, and Muhammad is His Messenger. *Lā ilāh illā Allāh Muḥammad Rasūl Allāh.*

My brothers and sisters in *Īmān-Islām,*[1] we have affirmed this *kalimah.*[2] We trust in God and have faith in Him alone, and with that determined faith we accept the revelations brought by the Prophet Muhammad. This is justice and truth, and truth is the silent witness in our life and in the hereafter.[3] To accept this truth and establish it is *Īmān-Islām.* To recite the *kalimah* to Allah with absolute faith, certitude, and determination, and to accept His representatives is *Īmān-Islām.* To pay obeisance to Him, to worship Him alone without the slightest doubt, to become His slave,[4] and to put His actions into practice in our lives is *Īmān-Islām.* From out of the beauty of Islam emerges Allah's power[5] and His wealth.

My brothers and sisters, before we consider the meaning of *jihād,* or holy war, let us think about the straight path and the oneness of Allah. This Unique, Almighty Power has no comparison; nothing is equal to Him, nothing can be likened to Him. That is why He is called the Incomparable One, and that is why we must accept Him.

---

1. *Īmān:* absolute faith, certitude, and determination.
   Islām: the state of absolute purity. See glossary.
2. *Lā ilāh illā Allāh Muḥammad Rasūl Allāh*
3. *al-ākhirah*
4. *'abd*
5. *qudrah*

The Qur'an, the traditions of the Prophet,[6] and the *kalimah* are His signs. They provide explanations about His representatives and about His power. The entire Qur'an is an explanation of the oneness of Allah, and the *kalimah* verifies this oneness. The Qur'an tells us with certainty that we are all the children of Adam and the slaves of Allah, our Creator. He is the One who gives according to the needs of each. He shows no differences among His creations; He creates, protects, and sustains us all. He is the Unique One who will call us all back and question us later. The Qur'an states this with certainty, and we must understand this with our seven states of wisdom. We who are the children of Adam must fully accept Him within our hearts. We must bow down[7] and prostrate[8] before Him. That is the meaning of the *kalimah* and the meaning of *Īmān-Islām.*

My brethren, let me tell you a story so that you may better understand the meaning of *jihād,* or holy war. When God formed Adam out of earth, He placed the great trust of the light of *Nūr Muḥammad* on Adam's forehead and decreed that man would know things that the angels and other beings could never know. The leader of the jinns was watching and listening. He became filled with jealousy, pride, and vengeance, and these qualities changed him into satan. At once he began to speak against God, boasting to Adam, "I am more exalted than you. Allah said that He created you to be most exalted, but you are only made of earth. I am made of fire. If you bow down to me I will help you, but if you attempt to rise above me, then I will do many evil things to you and make you suffer greatly."

Then that light on Adam's forehead looked closely at satan, and when satan saw the radiance, there arose within him an even greater fear, jealousy, and vengeance. Once again he sneered at Adam, "You are created out of mere earth, and yet you dare to look at me like this! Because you were given a higher place than I was, I will create sorrow and suffering for you until the very end." Then satan spat on him, and the moment that spit landed on Adam,

6. *aḥādīth*

7. *rukū'*

8. *sajdah*

satan's poisonous qualities entered him and spread throughout his entire body. Those qualities became the darkness of the mind and the veils within the innermost heart.

Upon seeing what had happened, Allah commanded the Angel Gabriel to pinch out that spot of hell where satan's spit had landed. The hollow that remained became the navel. Even though the spit itself was cleared away, some of the poison of those evil, envious qualities had already entered Adam and in that way were passed on to his descendents, causing all of mankind endless trouble. Because of satan's actions, Allah commanded that he and his followers be cast out of heaven. Then He elevated Adam to the high position decreed for him.

This is a very great matter. I have related only a small part of it to show you that the most important *jihād,* the holy war that each one of us must fight, is the war against these qualities. Just as satan was thrown out of heaven because he opposed the Almighty, Unique One, we too must cast out all that is evil within us, everything that opposes God. Those evil qualities of jealousy and vengeance are the qualities that ruin us and take us on the path to hell.

To help us fight this war, Allah sent us the *kalimah* and commanded us, "Recite this *kalimah* and cut away the enemy that is within you. Who is that enemy? Satan's evil qualities. They are an enemy to your body and to My unity and truth. Cut your connection to the evil one and cast out his qualities. Those qualities are the very fire of hell."

Therefore, with the *kalimah* and with Allah's qualities we must destroy the seven hells inside of us, and embrace instead the purity of the oneness of Allah. One who with wisdom and a pure heart accepts that oneness completely, also accepts the first *kalimah.* That is the affirmation of the unity of Allah,[9] and that is the first thing we have to do on the path of *Īmān-Islām.* We must accept this reality of the oneness of Allah without any doubt. This means that we must also accept everyone, all of Adam's children, as our brothers and sisters. We must think about this deeply, within our hearts.

The meaning of this is very, very profound. The purity we speak

---

9. *tawḥīd*

of is very deep. The state of absolute faith, certitude, and determination[10] is also deep, and from it comes the wisdom which will help us to understand these mysteries.

My brothers, the holy wars that the children of Adam are waging today are not true holy wars. Taking other lives is not true *jihād*. We will have to answer for that kind of war when we are questioned in the grave. That *jihād* is fought for the sake of men, for the sake of earth and wealth, for the sake of one's children, one's wife, and one's possessions. Selfish intentions are intermingled within it.

True *jihād* is to praise God and cut away the inner satanic enemies. When wisdom and clarity come to us, we will understand that the enemies of truth are within our own hearts. There are four hundred trillion, ten thousand spiritual opponents within the body: satan and his qualities of backbiting, deceit, jealousy, envy, treachery, the separations of I and you, mine and yours, intoxicants, theft, lust, murder, falsehood, arrogance, karma, illusion, mantras and magics, and the desire for earth, sensual pleasures, and gold. These are the enemies which separate us from Allah, from truth, from worship, from good actions and good thoughts, and from faith, certitude, and determination. These are the enemies which create divisions among the children of Adam and prevent us from attaining a state of peace.

Among the seventy-three groups of man, there are only a few who understand and fight the war against the enemy within themselves, the enemy who stands between them and Allah, the enemy who does not accept Allah and will not bow down and prostrate before Him. To cut our connection to this enemy who is leading us to hell is the true holy war.

Brothers, once we realize who is the foremost enemy of this treasure of truth which we have accepted, then we can begin our battle against that enemy. That is the holy war of faith, of the *kalimah*, and of Islam. That is the one holy war which Allah accepts.

We must not kill each other. Instead, we must wage war against the evil qualities within ourselves. When a child has bad qualities,

10. *īmān*

what does the mother do? She tries to teach him and help him to develop good qualities. Does she call him an evil child? No. If he steals the belongings of another because he wants to play with them, that is a bad quality no doubt, but the child is not evil. Does the mother strike down the child just because he has some bad qualities? No, the mother explains things to him and tries to expel the bad qualities and teach him good qualities. That is her duty, is it not?

Likewise, Allah, who created us, does not strike down His creations for the evil they have committed. It would not make sense if He did that. They are all His children, the children of the Lord of all creation. As their Father and Mother, He helps them to dispel their evil ways and tries to bring them to the straight path. He seeks to make His children happy and good. That is the way God is. And just as God does not kill His children because they have evil qualities, we must not murder others or cut them down. Instead, we must try to improve them by showing wisdom, love, compassion, and God's qualities, just as a mother teaches her mischievous child to change. That is our duty.

No good can come from cutting a person down. If a mother constantly shows unity and love to her child, that will get rid of the child's bad tendencies. In the same way, we must help others to remove the evil qualities, teach them good qualities, and lead them to the state where they can become the princes of God.

My brothers, if we act with love and unity, we can dispel all our evil qualities and live as one family, as one race, as children bowing to one Lord.[11] Once we understand this truth, we will become good children. But as long as we do not understand and do not cast off the evil, then we are bad children.

Of course, when you cut these qualities, it might hurt. It might cause difficulty and suffering. When a child is cut, the pain makes him cry. He may scream and fight or maybe even bite you. He may shout, "I will kill you!" But you must embrace him with love and patiently explain things to him, always remembering that the qualities within the child are the enemy, not the child himself.

---

11. *Rabb*

My brothers, man has two forms, each with its own set of qualities. The war is between these two forms. One is composed of the five elements and is ruled by the mind; it lives in the kingdom of illusion, creation, and hell. The other is a pure form made of Allah's light, of His resplendence and purity. That form lives in the kingdom of heaven, in the world of pure souls. When man dwells within this good form, he speaks and acts in good ways. When he moves into the form of the elements, he speaks and acts in evil ways. One body exists within him in a formless state; the other exists outside as his form and shadow. These two bodies have opposite qualities and duties.

The heart also has two sections: one is the innermost heart[12] and the other is the mind. The mind is connected to the fifteen worlds, which are ruled by the energies of earth, fire, water, air, and ether. Just as these five elements are mixed together in the earth and in the sky, they are also mingled within the body.

The fifteen worlds are connected to all of creation, to all forms. Seven of the worlds are above, seven are below, and the fifteenth world, which is the center, is the mind. It is there, in the world ruled by the mind, that the holy war must be waged. The mind and the energies of the elements roam up and down throughout the fifteen worlds, manifesting as the four hundred trillion, ten thousand miracles that create differences and divisions among men. We have to fight against all these energies in all fifteen worlds. This is the major battle. Once we complete this war, then we are ready to begin our work within the innermost heart.

The innermost heart is the kingdom of Allah. That is where His essence[13] can be found. The secret[14] of the eighteen thousand universes and the secret of this world are contained within that heart. Allah's messengers, His representatives, the angels, prophets, saints, the resplendently pure souls, and His light within the soul are all to be found in a tiny point within the heart. Within that atom is contained His entire kingdom, the kingdom of truth and

---

12. *qalb*

13. *dhāt*

14. *sirr*

justice and purity, the kingdom of heaven, the kingdom of enlightened wisdom.[15] The eighteen thousand universes are within that kingdom of light and divine knowledge,[16] and Allah is the ruler of all those universes. His infinite power, His three thousand gracious qualities, His ninety-nine attributes,[17] His compassion, peace, unity, and equality are all found within those universes. That is the innermost heart, His kingdom of true faith and justice, where one can find peace.

Until we reach that kingdom, we have to wage a holy war within ourselves. To show us how to cut away this enemy within and to teach us how to establish the connection with Him, Allah sent down 124,000 prophets, twenty-five of whom are described thoroughly in the Qur'an. These prophets came to teach us how to wage holy war against the inner enemy. This battle within should be fought with faith, certitude, and determination, with the *kalimah,* and with the Qur'an. No blood is shed in this war. Holding the sword of wisdom, faith, certitude, and justice, we must cut away the evil forces that keep charging at us in different forms. This is the inner *jihād.*

My brothers in *Īmān-Islām,* we must cut away the qualities which oppose Allah. There are no other enemies. Allah has no enemies. If anyone were to oppose Allah, the All-Powerful, Unique One, that person could never be victorious. You cannot raise or lower Allah. He does not accept praise or blame.

Praising Allah and then destroying others is not *jihād.* Some groups wage war against the children of Adam and call it holy war. But for man to raise his sword against man, for man to kill man, is not holy war. There is no point in that. There can be no benefit from killing a man in the name of God. Allah has no thought of killing or going to war. Why would Allah have sent His prophets if He had such thoughts? It was not to destroy men that Muhammad came; he was sent down as the wisdom that could show man how to destroy his own evil.

Once we have completely severed those qualities of satan within

15. *gnānam*

16. *'ilm*

17. *wilāyāt*

us, there will be no more enmity among human beings. All will live as brothers and sisters. That is true Islam, the affirmation of the unity of Allah, the oneness of Allah. Once we accept this, Allah accepts us. Once we fight and conquer these enemies of our faith, these enemies of our prayers, we will find peace within ourselves. And once we have found peace within, we will find peace everywhere. This world will be heaven, and we will have a direct connection to Allah, just as Adam had that original connection. Then we will understand the connection between ourselves and all the children of Adam.

Every child must know this and fight the enemy within. We must fight the battle between that which is permissible[18] under God's law and that which is forbidden.[19] If we do not do this, then the qualities of evil[20] will kill that which is good,[21] and the truth will be destroyed. But if we can win this huge battle, we will receive Allah's grace,[22] and that will enable us to know His eighteen thousand universes. If we can conquer the world of the mind, we will see the kingdom of the soul, His kingdom.

May every one of us think about this and wage our own holy war. Only when we finish the battle and progress beyond will we realize that we are all children of Adam, that we are all one race, that there is only one prayer, and that there is only One who is worthy of worship, one God, one Lord. He is the Compassionate One,[23] He is the Merciful One.[24] He creates and sustains all lives, He does not cut them down. Once we realize this, we will stop the fighting, the spilling of blood, the murder.

We will never attain peace and equality within our hearts until we finish this war, until we conquer the armies that arise from the thoughts and differences within ourselves, until we attack these enemies with faith, certitude, and determination and with patience, contentment, trust in God, and praise of God.[25] With divine

18. *ḥalāl*

19. *ḥarām*

20. *sharr*

21. *khayr*

22. *raḥmah*

23. *al-Raḥmān*

24. *al-Raḥīm*

25. *ṣabr, shukr, tawakkul 'alā Allāh,* and *al-ḥamdu lillāh*

knowledge, with justice and conscience, we must fight and win this inner *jihād*.

May the peace of God be with you.[26] Allah is sufficient for all. Amen.

26. *al-salām 'alaykum*

صبر شكر

توكل على الله الحمد لله

Ṣabr

Inner patience

Shukr

Contentment

Tawakkul ʻalá Allāh

Trust in God

Al-ḥamdu lillāh

Praise of God

Once we understand what the true weapons of Islam are, we will never take a life, we will never even see anyone as separate from ourselves. We will not be able to conceive of any enmity. We will realize that each and every one of us must act in accordance with Allah's actions and with the same inner patience, contentment, trust in God, and praise of God shown by the Prophet Muhammad.

THE WEAPONS OF ISLAM

أعوذ بالله من الشيطان الرجيم   بسم الله الرحمن الرحيم

I seek refuge in Allah from the evils of the accursed satan.
In the name of Allah, Most Merciful, Most Compassionate.

May the peace of God be upon all my brothers and sisters[1] in *Īmān-Islām*.[2] May all responsibility be offered to God, the Most Exalted One,[3] the Unfathomable Ruler of Grace who is incomparable love. Amen. You alone are responsible for the Day of Questioning[4] and the Day of Judgment, for the beginning of life and the time of death, for life in this world and the next. You confer the grace,[5] ask the questions, and give the judgment. You are the mercy and compassion for all the universes.[6] Amen.

O Allah, You are the light and the plenitude of the grace of perfect purity.[7] May You be the protector of the people of purity. May You make that purity the complete, never-ending wealth of grace in the innermost hearts[8] of those who are on the path of the light of faith, certitude, and determination.[9] May You show them the way and give them Your grace. Amen.

O Allah, may You help all those who have received the grace of Islam and have made that grace their never-ending wealth. May they never lose their way on the path of purity. May You reveal the true path to them, and may they proceed on that path to Your

---

1. *al-salām 'alaykum*
2. *Īmān:* absolute faith, certitude, and determination.
   Islām: the state of absolute purity. See glossary.
3. *Allāh ta'āla'*
4. *Qiyāmah*
5. *raḥmah*
6. *raḥmat al-'ālamīn*
7. *dīn*
8. *qalb*
9. *īmān*

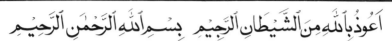

heavenly paradise.[10] Amen. May You grant those of purity the undiminishing wealth of Your grace. Amen.

May the peace, the beneficence, and the blessings of God be upon you. I give greetings of peace to all of my very precious brothers, my exalted brothers who are one through the light of the Qur'an and who have been given the wealth of perfect faith, my brothers who are great and wise in Islam, who have received the wealth of unending life, the eternal life[11] of absolute faith. To all my eight hundred million brothers in Islam I give my humble greetings of peace.

Allah sent 124,000 prophets to explain His laws and codes of behavior and to give us the weapons needed to fight the huge battle in our hearts. Of those 124,000 prophets, He chose twenty-five and sent them bearing His sound and His revelations.[12] To reveal His truth and strengthen our faith, Allah gave these messengers the holy words of grace for all three worlds. He sent them so that each heart would open and develop faith, certitude, and determination. Every prophet told us to love Allah, to accept Him with determined faith, and to worship and pray to Him without any racial or religious prejudice.

It was to bring this message that God, the Most Exalted, sent so many prophets through His holy grace. Then He made His resonance into the teachings of the Holy Qur'an and sent that to the Final Prophet, Muhammad, the Chosen Messenger.[13] Through the Angel Gabriel, Allah revealed to Muhammad His words, His actions, His conduct, His goodness, and His powers.[14] We must reflect deeply upon every explanation contained within this Holy Qur'an, which exists in all three realms: the primal beginning, this world, and the hereafter.[15]

We who are the community of Islam must remember that ultimately, everything was given to Islam. What was given? God,

---

10. *firdaws*
11. *ḥayāh*
12. *waḥy*
13. *Muḥammad Muṣṭafā al-Rasūl*
14. *wilāyāt*
15. *al-awwal, dunyā,* and *al-ākhirah*

the Most Exalted, gave formal prayer[16] to Islam as a weapon for this world and the next. He ordained that the fifty times of prayer, or *waqts,* be made into five. With inner patience, contentment, trust in God, and giving all praise to God,[17] we must use this weapon of prayer to fight the inner war and eliminate the enmity and hatred within ourselves. We must dispel our base desires,[18] our prejudices, our religious and racial differences, the countless demons and ghosts of arrogance, and the karma and illusion within our bodies. Pride, jealousy, the sense of separation between men, and all other evils must be fought with this weapon which the Messenger of God brought and offered as the final teaching to those who are on the path of perfect purity.

In addition to the five-times prayer, God Almighty ordained the five obligatory duties[19] for the Muslim community. These too are weapons of Islam which help us to overcome hell, satan, and evil qualities. The first obligatory duty is to surrender to Allah with absolute faith. For those who do this with perfect certitude, the second duty is to worship Allah alone, without thinking for a moment that He might have any equal or any partner. Those with such faith glorify the name of Allah in every one of their 43,242 breaths inhaled and exhaled daily. Their focus is on Allah alone. Allah is their grace, their soul, their food, and their wealth. Such people are known as the seventy-third group.

Of the seventy-three groups of mankind who are the descendants of Adam, only that one group with perfect faith is in a state of pure Islam. Of the other seventy-two groups, seventy have no faith in Allah. The two remaining groups do accept and worship Allah, but they also have a selfish desire for the world and a love of earth, gold, and sensual pleasures.

Allah addresses these two groups in the Qur'an: "You who have accepted perfect faith! Whatever wealth you have does not belong to you, it belongs to Allah. Therefore, give charity to those who are in need, feed the hungry, take care of those with difficulties, share the

---

16. *ṣalāh*

17. *ṣabr, shukr, tawakkul 'alá Allāh,* and *al-ḥamdu lillāh*

18. *nafs*

19. *furūḍ*

food and nourishment of Allah with others." This is the third duty, that of true charity,[20] which was made obligatory for those two groups of people, so they would recognize the lives of others to be as valuable as their own and comfort and care for them as they would for themselves.

But for those who did not observe the third duty correctly or understand its full significance, Allah ordained the fourth duty of fasting[21] so that they might come to a realization of the suffering of others. Allah told them to undertake a compulsory fast of thirty days in succession and an optional fast of ten more days. The purpose of fasting is to become aware of your own hunger pangs and your own suffering. That is true fasting. If you understand that, you will share your food and wealth with your brothers.

But because this duty was not observed or understood correctly either, Allah ordained the fifth duty of pilgrimage.[22] True pilgrimage is to enter the state of dying before death. For the poor, who cannot afford to go to Mecca, pilgrimage means gathering together for the traditional Friday noontime prayers[23] in their own town or city. For the rich, pilgrimage means going to Mecca and Medina. Before making this journey the pilgrim must give away all possessions, return his wife's dowry, distribute his wealth, and be dead to the world. He is even clothed in a white shroud like a corpse.

Charity, fasting, and pilgrimage—these three duties were made obligatory for those who had not fully comprehended the first two duties, to have faith in God and His Messenger and to worship only God. However, those in the seventy-third group have nothing to give. The only things they receive from Allah are His grace and the wisdom and comfort of the Qur'an and the traditions of the Prophet.[24] Since these are all that they receive, these are all that they can give as charity.

The seventy-third group goes directly to heaven without any judgment, but the other two groups will have to face the Day of

---

20. *zakāh*

21. *ṣawm*

22. *ḥajj*

23. *jum'ah*

24. *aḥādīth*

Questioning. For them there is a Judgment Day. For the other seventy groups there is the hell of the world. The Qur'an and the traditions of the Prophet give evidence of this.

My brothers in Islam, beyond these five outer weapons, Allah has also given us six inner weapons, which the Sufis have explained. If you go deep into Allah with the certitude of unwavering faith, you will see that within this eye of yours is an inner eye which can gaze upon Allah. Within this nostril is a piece of flesh which can smell the fragrance of Allah. Within this ear is a piece of flesh which can hear the sounds of Allah. Within this tongue is a piece of flesh which can taste the beauty and the divine knowledge of Allah and know the taste of His wealth.[25] Within this tongue is also a voice which converses with Him and recites His remembrance[26] in a state of total absorption.

Within this innermost heart is a piece of flesh where the eighteen thousand universes, the heavens, and His kingdom are found. And there the angels, the heavenly beings, prophets, and lights of Allah prostrate before Him. Allah's throne,[27] His gnostic eye,[28] His justice, and the divine pen[29] are there in His palace, where He rules and passes judgment. And in that palace is an inscription saying, "There is no god but God. He is the One who rules the universe,[30] the world of the souls,[31] and all of everything."

This piece of flesh within the heart contains the wisdom[32] which can discover that palace of Allah. It is the wisdom of His divine knowledge, and the clarity of it permits us to realize everything and to understand Him and bow down before Him, glorifying His name with each of the 43,242 daily outgoing and incoming breaths.

So much is contained in this innermost heart of man, which is the throne of the true believer.[33] Only when we understand all this, will we fully comprehend the essence of the six inner duties.

---

25. *dawlah*

26. *dhikr*

27. *'arsh*

28. *kursī*

29. *qalam*

30. *'ālam*

31. *'ālam al-arwāḥ*

32. *ḥikmah*

33. *'arsh al-mu'min*

We who are in Islam must understand and act in accordance with both the inner and outer duties. These are truly great weapons, and with them we must fight the battle within. We must overcome everything in our hearts that covers the truth, all that reflects our disbelief.[34] We must overcome our infidel minds, our infidel thoughts, our infidel hearts. We must dispel all disbelief and stop the eating of forbidden[35] foods and other such acts. We must overcome the darkness that gives way to pride, jealousy, vengeance, treachery, and trickery. We must discard the magic of illusion and unreality. God Almighty sent these weapons to us through His Messenger so that we would be able to overcome all the evils that are overcoming us.

My precious brothers in the community of Islam, who have been granted absolute faith and have received Allah's wealth and grace[36] and blessing of perfect purity in all three worlds—all my brothers who are within that purity—these are the weapons that were given to the Messenger of God, and they are also our weapons. To put them to use is Islam. These are the weapons for those who are of the pure faith known as Islam.

Each person in Islam must understand where this real war must be fought, where the real battlefield exists. Each must understand what it is that is dividing and destroying Islam, what it is that is denying Allah and breaking up His kingdom. Each must understand the nature of jealousy, the nature of pride, and the nature of that selfishness which says, "Mine!" To cut away all these things, Allah sent us the weapons of the five times of prayer, the five obligatory duties, and the strength of inner patience, contentment, trust in God, and giving all praise to God. This is the final message given to Prophet Muhammad.

My brothers who are in the community of Islam, to further our understanding of these teachings we must reflect upon the life of the

---

34. *kufr*

35. *ḥarām*

36. *barakat*

Prophet. When Abū Jahl, Ikrimah, Ḥabīb Ibn Mālik,[37] and others who opposed Muhammad chased him out of Mecca, they caused him great suffering. They even tried to kill him. We must realize that they did this because they kept their gods of the past within themselves—their mantras, their magics, their family gods, their idols, and their satans, some of which could talk. In the darkness of their worship, they made offerings and sacrifices to these idols of darkness. They worshiped forty-eight thousand idols, three hundred and sixty of which could be seen housed in the *Ka'bah*.[38]

At that time, the fire of satan, the pride of satan, and the qualities of satan were alive, manifesting as the anger of man. So God sent the light of Muhammad to fight that darkness. And when Muhammad came as the light, the darkness became his enemy, chasing him and his companions[39] from Mecca to Medina. But the companions had prayer, and they had inner patience, contentment, trust in God, and praise of God. Allah said to them, "These are the weapons which will cut through the darkness and overcome enmity. They will overcome the separations, egoism, and prejudices present in the minds that are filled with disbelief. These weapons are a radiant light which will sever the darkness and prove that Allah alone exists."

Allah gave these weapons to His Messenger, telling him, "O Muhammad, say, 'There is no god other than God. There is no one worthy of worship other than God, the Most Exalted.' Teach the people this *kalimah*. That is why I sent it to you. Explain it to them,

---

37. Abū Jahl: One of the foremost adversaries of Muhammad. His real name was 'Amr Ibn Misham but the Muslims nicknamed him Abū Jahl, or the "Father of Ignorance." Ikrimah: The son of Abū Jahl. For many years, along with his father, he was a determined opponent of Muhammad. However he later embraced Islam and became a companion of the Prophet. Ḥabīb Ibn Mālik: A prince of the major Arabian tribes who was asked by Abū Jahl to question Muhammad in the hope of proving him a false prophet. According to some narratives, Muhammad performed several miracles, including the splitting of the moon (referred to in the 54th chapter of the Qur'an), thus convincing Ḥabīb and converting him to Islam.
38. The cube-like building in the center of the mosque in Mecca.
39. *aṣḥāb*

and tell them to accept Me.

"Explain to them that the primal beginning, this world, and the hereafter are My kingdom. I am the Ruler, I am the Judge, I alone provide the food for the living and the dead, and I am the One who will ask the questions on Judgment Day. I am the One who judges. Teach this to the people."

So that Allah's commandments would be accepted, Muhammad sent these words to every nation. He told them, "Almighty God is the Ruler of Grace. He has no children, no relations, no comparison, no equal. He is the Eternal One, the Omnipresent, Eternal Ruler, who guides us along the true path."

Muhammad spread these words throughout the land, by way of his couriers. Some people accepted Allah, but others did not. The kingdoms where Allah was not accepted were destroyed by fire, by water, by hurricane, by battle, and by the arrogance and pride of the people. Destruction came and lands were covered by oceans, cities became jungles, and villages became cemeteries. But every place which accepted Allah was under His safekeeping and became the kingdom of God, the kingdom of perfect faith.

Abū Jahl and his followers were among those who did not accept Allah's message, and it was because of them that the battles of Badr and Uhud[40] were fought and many people were killed. But those battles were not fought to conquer other nations. They were fought to conquer the qualities of satan which refused to accept Allah. They were battles between the truth of Allah and falsehood. They were fought so that people could pray, worship, and accept His judgment, and so that justice would prevail.

It would be very good if every heart among the eight hundred

40. The battle of Badr was fought between the followers of Muhammad and those among the Quraysh who rejected the belief in Allah and Muhammad. Many of Islam's principle opponents were killed, including Abū Jahl. The victory of Badr established the ability of the Muslims to defend themselves. The battle of Uhud was also between the followers of Muhammad and the Quraysh. The outcome of the battle was mixed, the Muslims being outflanked by Khālid Ibn al-Walīd, a great warrior among the Quraysh who later embraced Islam. The Quraysh, however, did not pursue their advantage and were forced to retreat by the regrouped Muslims.

million people of Islam understood this. Muhammad did not fight to usurp land or gold or to capture women. The commandments of Allah tell us not to try to rule the world, but instead to rule the innermost heart of a true human being,[41] the place known as the throne of the true believer, His kingdom. Allah is the only One who can rule that kingdom. He rules each heart with the wealth of the mercy of all the universes, with His justice, His patience, and His attributes. Anyone who can rule in this manner is a true ruler. Whether he is a political leader, one who leads the prayers,[42] or a learned teacher,[43] the one who can rule the hearts of the people is the exalted true believer,[44] the God-realized being.[45]

My brothers, we must use patience to acquire those qualities which can rule the heart, for that is the greatest kingdom of all, and to govern there is the most exalted rulership. Those who do not govern the people's hearts, but instead rule over the earth, really govern in hell. Such things belong to hell and to the curse of hell.[46] Pride is hell, and the attractions of earth, gold, sensual pleasures, and possessions are advertisements that lure us to the seven hells. To overcome those hells we must begin to govern the heart with good qualities, with prayer, and with worship.[47] Those who are in Islam must realize this.

The wars during the time of the Prophet were fought so that truth would be accepted, but the wars we are engaged in today are being fought for the sake of conquering nations, capturing countries, and killing and vanquishing others. This is not the kind of war that true Islam wages. Each of us must remember this. We must realize that it is not right for us to display such hostility. Patience and compassion are appropriate for us. We must realize that it is not right for us to harbor hatred. Contentment is appropriate for us at all times, in all circumstances. We must realize that it is not right for us

41. *insān*

42. *imām*

43. *'ālim*

44. *mu'min*

45. *insān kāmil*

46. *la'nat al-jahannam*

47. *'ibādah*

to be angry, because anger belongs to satan. Only absolute trust in God is appropriate for Islam. We must give all praise to Allah for the food that we eat between each time of prayer.[48] We must say, ''All praise be to God,'' for everything we receive in our lives, whether it be a great feast or a glass of water, immense wealth or dire poverty. To praise Allah at each moment, no matter what happens, is Islam.

Enmity cannot be overcome with enmity. Each of you must realize that in true Islam enmity does not exist. If you see someone else as your enemy, it is your own reflection that you are seeing. Hostility cannot be overcome by hostility; to overcome it, you must first rid yourself of your own hostility and then have inner patience. Vengeance cannot be defeated by vengeance; if you want to defeat it, you must first overcome your own vengeance and then practice love and compassion. You must do this with inner patience, contentment, trust in God, and giving all praise to God. Jealousy cannot be overcome by jealousy. It was because of satan's jealousy that he ruined Adam. If you let that quality grow within yourself, you can never subdue it in others. However, if you can overcome your own jealousy with compassion, patience, and contentment, then you can help others to overcome theirs.

Hatred cannot be overcome by hatred, nor anger by anger. Anger is fire, and God created the jinns and their leader, satan, out of that fire. Because of his hatred and anger, satan was hurled from heaven into this world of hell. Anyone who has that anger in him is a satan. If we are angry, we will see anger in others, but if we overcome satan's anger in ourselves, we will not see it in anyone else.

It is our own satanic qualities that must be overcome with inner patience, contentment, trust in God, and giving all praise to God. However, if instead we nourish these evil qualities, then Allah will throw us away from Himself. Just as He cast off satan, He will throw us out of heaven into hell.

In this world there are four hundred trillion, ten thousand spiritual energies given shape by satan's magic, his trickery, and his treachery. They are found in the earth, air, fire, water, and ether of

---

48. *waqt*

the body. If we can overcome these evil energies within ourselves, then we can see heaven there. And if heaven exists within us, we can embrace everyone equally. We can have compassion for everyone and be loving, tolerant, peaceful, and patient to everyone. We can be filled with contentment, trust in God, and praise of God and receive Allah's grace. This must be realized within the innermost heart of everyone in Islam.

My brothers, once we understand what the true weapons of Islam are, we will never take a life, we will not murder, we will not even see any brother as separate from ourselves. We will not be able to conceive of any enmity. Almighty God revealed and explained this state to His Messenger, and we who are in Islam must understand. When we do, we will know Allah and His state as revealed in the ninety-nine attributes of Allah's ninety-nine beautiful names.[49] We will realize that each and every one of us must act in accordance with Allah's actions and with the same patience, contentment, trust in God, and praise of God shown by His Messenger. Patience and the three thousand beautiful qualities of Allah are the mercy and compassion for all the universes and the wealth of Islam. If we have this, we will not feel hatred or hostility for anyone or for any nation.

God, the Most Exalted, gave this world to everyone. In a direct revelation[50] to Muhammad, Allah said, "The eighth heaven is My nation, and everyone who comes here belongs to one family. I dispense judgment, and there are no separations here, no differences of color, religion, race, language, or scripture. There is only one place for everyone who accepts Me. In the eighth heaven you are all the children of Adam. Each of you will have a place in accordance with the way you search for Me. I will give you your appropriate rewards."

All who are great and wise in the community of Islam, the rulers and those who serve the rulers, the teachers,[51] the saints,[52] and the great holy men of divine wisdom[53] must know that Almighty God has

49. *Asmā' al-ḥusnā*

50. *ḥadīth qudsī*

51. *'ulamā'*

52. *awliyā'*

53. *quṭbs*

given to each of His creations the appropriate place at the appropriate time. He gave the snake its hole and the ant its anthill. He made places for the reptiles and for the birds. He gave the jinns and fairies places to live, He gave the angels and heavenly beings places, and He even gave a place to satan and to evil. He made room for both light and darkness, for that which is permissible[54] according to God's law and for that which is forbidden.[55] He made room for everyone. He made separate places for men and beasts so that each would have his own particular dwelling. Almighty God provided a place for all the children of Adam, for all the children of every religion, race, and language. And in the same way, Allah provided a place for each prophet.

Islam does not usurp that which was given to another by God; it neither destroys nor takes anyone else's place. There is no room in Islam for hurting others, taking their possessions or their homes. Islam sees its neighbors as brothers, not as different or separate. It does not kill others. It shows them love, compassion, and patience, and gives them the wealth of absolute faith, patience, contentment, and trust in God. True Islam brings only peace; it contains no enmity whatsoever. We who are in Islam must realize this and know that Almighty God has given to every creation a place, a country, a spouse, a treasure, or a kingdom. We must be content and say, "Allah is responsible for everything.[56] All praise is due to Him alone."

It is our responsibility to accept Allah and the teachings of His Messenger. But over the last hundred years some people of Islam and of other religions have changed. Faith has decreased to the point where many say that God does not exist. The darkness and torpor of desire for earth, gold, and sensual pleasures have entered our hearts and changed us. We must dispel this darkness from our innermost hearts. The satanic qualities of jealousy, vengeance, anger, sin, and pride have come into us. The Messenger of God

54. *ḥalāl*

55. *ḥarām*

56. *tawakkul 'alá Allāh*

chased all these away from us before, but now they have returned.

We must strengthen our faith and using the weapons of the five-times prayer and of patience, contentment, trust in God, and praise of God, we must once again chase away those evil qualities from our hearts. Our job is not to chase others from their homes, or wage war against others, or kill them, or cause them pain, because they too are the children of Adam. We who are in Islam must never hurt anyone. We have to understand this. The words and traditions of the Prophet and the explanations of the Qur'an tell us very clearly the way we must live. I humbly plead with you to do this. True Islam must be reestablished and receive again the wealth of prayer. You and I, all of us, must live entirely in a state of inner patience, contentment, absolute trust in God, and giving all praise to God.

Over fourteen hundred years ago Allah sent the purity of Islam to the Prophet Muhammad, the Chosen Messenger of the Almighty God. There is a traditional story about this. Some of the companions of the Prophet asked how long that purity of Islam would last in the world, and he said, "The purity will be protected for fourteen hundred years. During that time it will be safe, but we must surrender what comes afterwards to Allah. He alone knows what will happen to Islam."

That time is now! Those fourteen hundred years have passed. Today is the time the Prophet was referring to. Put your trust in God. He alone knows the fate of Islam. If we look at what is happening in Islam today, we will be able to understand why this was said. Faith in Allah and focus on Him have decreased tremendously. Islam no longer seems to understand the difference between what is permissible according to God's law and what is forbidden, nor the difference between good and evil, right and wrong, or truth and falsehood. Islamic people have turned to war and fighting. They no longer appear to fear the Day of Questioning or even the Day of Judgment. Wherever we look, we see Islamic nations allying themselves with those who have no faith in God, with those who deny God. They have turned to tigers and to the enemies of Allah for help.

We who are in Islam must remember that Allah is our only helper every second, every minute, every hour, every time of prayer. Allah is our Ruler, the Ruler of Grace, the One who is Love, the Compassionate One, the One who calls us back to Him, the One who questions us, and the One who judges us. His grace exists in all lives, concealed in a tiny piece of flesh within the innermost heart. Just as the flesh of the tongue knows taste, just as the flesh of the nose perceives smell and the flesh of the ear hears sound and the flesh of the eye perceives light—like that, there is a tiny piece of flesh in the heart which worships Allah, looks at Him, hears Him, and prays to Him.

This is the throne of the true believer. This is where Allah dwells. This is His throne within the innermost heart, from which He rules and dispenses justice. It is the seat of judgment in this world and the next. That piece of flesh, that light, that grace, discerns the difference between good and evil without our ever being aware of it. In the same way that our senses perceive physical things, it discerns good and evil in whatever the eyes see, the nose smells, the ears hear, and the tongue tastes. It discerns the good and evil in our thoughts and intentions. This tiny piece of flesh is hidden within the body of the elements, but it cannot be destroyed by earth, fire, air, or water. It is this which will rise on the Day of Questioning.

To make it possible to discover this secret, Almighty God placed the radiance of *Nūr Muḥammad*[57] in the throne on the crown of the head, resplending there as the wisdom of man. Each heart has a scale which uses wisdom to weigh good and evil, to judge right and wrong. We must attach the trays of: 'There is nothing other than You, O God,' and: 'Only You are Allah.' to the scale of perfect faith and put everything we collect in our lives on either the left or the right tray. Instead of nourishing hostility or evil, we should avoid them. We should place them on the left side of the scale. Then we must read the gauge, the indicator of wisdom, so we can eliminate

57. The light which became completeness within Allah and then emerged.

the evil and gather up the good.

This is judgment, and Islam must understand this judgment. If we understand right and wrong and good and evil in this world, if we understand them with absolute faith, with the *kalimah,* and with the qualities of Allah, we will push away every bad thing and do only what is right. We will rid ourselves of all that is evil. Then we can put Allah's wealth of truth in our treasury, where complete trust in God and praise of Him exist. Each heart must think about this.

Īmān-Islām must give the treasures of satan to satan and the treasures of Allah to Allah. With trust and surrender to God, Islam must gather up the treasures of truth. But today in Islam, we have forgotten Allah. We have tried to rule the world, forfeiting the wealth of Allah and instead accepting the wealth of the world. We have begun to consider earth, gold, and sensual pleasures as our wealth, even though they can all be destroyed in a second by an earthquake, a hurricane, or a storm.

When Abraham was put into a fiery pit, he sought the help of Allah alone. He would not ask for anyone else's help. If those of us who have absolute faith also seek only His help, that treasure of grace will be endless. But if we seek the world and its material treasures, those things will change and leave us one day. The land will be covered by oceans, cities will be turned into forests, and villages will become cemeteries. Worldly wealth changes that way and is finally destroyed.

Everyone in Islam who has absolute faith, certitude, and determination must know this and accept it. We must earn that wealth, instead of trying to capture the wealth of the world. The treasures in our lives must be inner patience, contentment, trust in God, and praise of God, along with prayer, worship, remembrance of God, and contemplation.[58] We must have Allah's three thousand gracious, beautiful qualities and His ninety-nine attributes. We must use each action which Allah revealed to us in His beautiful names. If we do, Islam will never be destroyed, it will never be degraded, and it will never be in danger. We must realize this and fill ourselves with patience so that we can overcome any enmity

58. *ṣalāh, 'ibādah, dhikr,* and *fikr*

within us.

Everyone filled with the light of faith must reflect on this. True Islam means cutting away all hostility within ourselves, embracing everyone in brotherhood, uniting congregation with congregation. We must remember that on the Day of Questioning, all the children of Adam will become one congregation in heaven, in paradise, in the kingdom of Allah. Everyone in Islam must remember this.

If we all accepted and understood this, we would not fight. We would know that our only enemies are those who do not accept Allah, those who deny Allah and see Him as their enemy. Islam is not war, it is not murder, it is not battles. This is not what we must engage in. Peace is Islam, patience is Islam, contentment is Islam, trust in God is Islam, the praise of God is Islam. Love is Islam. This is the umbrella, the canopy of goodness which God Almighty sent to Muhammad, His Chosen Messenger. Having received it from Allah, he gave it to us. If we fill our innermost hearts with this love, then no hatred, no battle, no bloodshed will ever befall us. If we understand this, we will see peace in the whole world. Radiance, light, and truth will illuminate our lives and our hearts.

The Qur'an has protected those with absolute faith since the Prophet first came. Not one drop of blood of the prophets, or of the true believers who are the perfect followers of Muhammad, or of those who are in *Īmān-Islām* may be spilled on this earth. Indeed, the earth will not drink the blood of those who have accepted perfect faith and the light of perfect purity. But if the blood of those lights of Allah should ever be shed, then the land in which that crime occurred would be completely destroyed.

My brothers, we have not come here to shed blood. Those with faith have not come for that. We have come to make peace between the world and heaven, the world and eternity. We have come here to live in peace, with patience. We have come to implant the grace and light of faith in each heart and to open the path to the eighth heaven. With the qualities of Prophet Muhammad and the qualities and actions of the ninety-nine attributes of Allah as examples, we must offer peace and comfort to everyone and try to take each one of our brothers along the straight, true path.

Our true state is peace; our true state is inner patience, contentment, trust in God, and praise of God. This is the grace of Islam, the wealth of our life. Once we understand this grace and behave as those in Islam should, all the creatures of land and sea, the jinns and fairies, each and every one of Allah's creations will prostrate before that light and worship that beauty of Islam. If we trust in God completely and surrender all responsibility to Him, everything will subordinate itself to Islam and prostrate to that purity. Except for satan, there is no opposition to true Islam. All others will prostrate themselves. This is shown with perfect clarity and perfect resplendence in the Qur'an, which came to us as Allah's resonance and was explained to us by His Messenger. Each one of us who has faith and certitude must realize this true state and then help others to change.

People need water to survive; even if there is no food to eat they must at least have water. The grace of Allah is the water of *Īmān-Islām*. When you see someone starving for that water of grace, you must give him some, revive him, take him away from the sufferings of the world, nurture his life, change his state, and help him to follow God's laws.

My brothers, you must quench the thirst of all lives with that grace and let them rest. You must try to heal the sufferings of the world. This is the mercy and compassion of all the universes, the wealth that has been given to mankind, and we who have faith must strive to offer it to all. We should not carry a sword in our hands; we should hold patience in our hearts. We should not arm ourselves with guns; we should be armed with contentment. We should not put our trust in battles; we should have trust in God. We should not cling to the world; we should cling to the praise of God. These are the true weapons of Islam.

My brothers in Islam, all the leaders of the world, all the learned, exalted people of wisdom who have faith in the Qur'an, all who believe in Allah and in His Messenger, all who have the right to the dignity of Islam—all of you must bring peace to the world. Chase away the arrogance, darkness, and demons that lurk in the heart. With the weapons of love, patience, and contentment, conquer those hearts and unite them under the umbrella of Islam, under the flag of *Īmān-Islām,* under the light of Muhammad. Those hearts will melt and prostrate to that love. The Prophet had no warlike qualities. He had only the qualities of patience, contentment, trust in God, and praise of God. If those qualities are reestablished in each heart, if they flourish and grow there, then Islam will become a vast, protective canopy for the world.

If everyone in the community of Islam understood this and tried to establish peace, tolerance, and patience, that alone would bring peace to the world. The weapons of peace and tranquility will grant us victory no matter what enmity, what hostility, threatens us. We must realize this, my brothers in Islam. If we do, we will triumph in all three worlds, in the primal beginning, this world, and the hereafter.

In the name of Allah and His Messenger, I beg you to forgive me if anything I have said is wrong. Please forgive me if I have made any mistakes. I am only telling you what came to my heart. I am only telling you what I understand in my innermost heart.

I humbly ask the great, the wise, and the learned ones to do this. If there is any fault in what I have said, please forgive me for the sake of Allah and His Messenger. May all the peace, the beneficence, and the blessings of God be upon you. Amen.

الله اكبر

Allāh Akbar

God is Most Great

Do not shout, ''Allāh Akbar! *God is Most Great!'' and then kill someone. Instead, lead him to the good path, the straight path, and say,* ''Allāh Akbar!'' *He is the Almighty One who can create and destroy within the blinking of an eye. Life and death belong to Him, not to us.*

THE LAWS OF HOLY WAR

أَعُوذُ بِاللّٰهِ مِنَ الشَّيْطَانِ الرَّجِيمِ بِسْمِ اللّٰهِ الرَّحْمٰنِ الرَّحِيمِ

I seek refuge in Allah from the evils of the accursed satan.
In the name of Allah, Most Merciful, Most Compassionate.

My brothers and sisters in *Īmān-Islām,*[1] let us speak further on the meaning of holy war, or *jihād.*

If we understand the Qur'an properly, and if we understand the traditions of the Prophet,[2] then Islam will be the water of grace[3] for the entire world. It will cleanse everyone of their dirt and quench their thirst. It will make all hearts peaceful and be the very pulse of life, the heartbeat for all the children of Adam, for all of creation.

A direct revelation[4] *to Muhammad, the Messenger of God*[5]

The exalted Prophet, his companions,[6] and his followers were constantly being attacked by those who did not accept Allah or His Messenger. With forbearance and contentment, Muhammad tolerated all the suffering that came to him, and he conveyed to his followers the patience and the trust in Allah that was given to him. However, eventually it became necessary to escape from this persecution, and he and his followers fled to Medina. Many of the people of Medina immediately accepted the Prophet, and there he and his followers found some peace. But a few hypocrites and troublemakers traveled between the two cities, spreading rumors,

---

1. *Īmān:* absolute faith, certitude, and determination.
   Islām: the state of absolute purity. See glossary.
2. *aḥādīth*
3. *raḥmah*
4. *ḥadīth qudsī*
5. *Rasūl Allāh*
6. *aṣḥāb*

backbiting, and creating enmity. "The people of Mecca want to fight you," they told the Prophet and his followers. "They are destroying your homes and all the property that you left behind. They are killing your wives and children and injuring your brothers."

Upon hearing these stories, some of the companions complained to the Prophet pleading, "O *Rasūl,*[7] they are causing us so much suffering! They have harmed our families, taken our possessions, destroyed our homes, and chased us from place to place. And now they are calling us cowards for running away. But we are courageous warriors and must live with honor and dignity. We have accepted this disgrace long enough. Now we must fight!

"You are the Messenger of Allah. This world and the hereafter[8] are one to you, and Allah is sufficient for you as your only wealth. So you are not concerned if people try to disgrace you, but in our state we cannot bear this. We need the means to live in this world as well as in the hereafter. The Meccans have destroyed our houses, our property, and our relations. We must fight to regain our possessions, for our hearts are hurt and we are suffering."

The companions of the Prophet pleaded like this time after time. But Muhammad did not grant them permission to fight. His heart was crying. The light in his eyes looked toward Allah and his hands were outstretched asking for perfect faith and the wealth[9] of Allah's divine knowledge. He spent every moment in this state, asking Allah to change the hearts of the people. The only sword in his hand was the sword of love and unity, the sword of faith, certitude, and determination, the sword of patience, contentment, trusting God, and praise of God.

Then, after a while, Ḥamzah[10] came with the same request, but the Prophet would not yield to him either. He would not tell his followers to begin a holy war. Instead, he always answered, "You

---

7. The resplendent Messenger of God.

8. *dunyā* and *al-ākhirah*

9. *dawlah*

10. Ḥamzah: The paternal uncle and foster brother of the Prophet.

cannot do this without Allah's permission, and Allah has not granted it. Therefore, I cannot give you my permission either. The true holy war of Islam is a war against our base desires[11] and against all those aspects within ourselves which are the real enemies to our life in the hereafter."

But still his companions pleaded, "We are warriors, and we have been disgraced. How can we live in this world with such dishonor?"

Then, while the Prophet waited silently, Allah's answer came. "O Muhammad, tell your companions to begin the holy war in their hearts, to sacrifice the evils in their own hearts. Your companions need to understand this."

The Prophet conveyed this to his companions. "My brothers, Allah has said that if you want to begin a holy war, your first duty is to wage that war against the army of enemies that harm you from within. Each one of you must make your heart acceptable to Him. You must make your heart pure according to God's law by performing the ritual sacrifice[12] needed to destroy the evils which come to destroy you. You must cut away all the things that occlude your heart. Make your heart light. Nourish it with the food of light which is the treasure of Allah, and avoid all that is forbidden."[13]

Allah told His Messenger, "Only one who partakes of My food will have his hunger and his desires appeased. The permissible[14] food for the heart consists of My divine knowledge,[15] My ninety-nine attributes,[16] My qualities and actions, My patience and contentment, surrender to Me, trusting Me, and praising Me alone.[17] Only such praise will end his hunger. With My angels I will protect anyone who makes this intention the light within his heart, anyone who understands each of these three thousand gracious qualities, anyone in whom these qualities emerge.

"O Muhammad, I will reveal to you the angels that will come to

---

11. *nafs*

12. *qurbān*

13. *ḥarām*

14. *ḥalāl*

15. *'ilm*

16. *wilāyāt*

17. *ṣabr, shukr, tawakkul 'alá Allāh,* and *al-ḥamdu lillāh*

protect you from the armies of Ḥabīb Ibn Mālik, sent by Abū Jahl.[18] Each angel will have three thousand heads and six thousand hands, and will wield the weapons appropriate to them. You will be able to see them all. So even if you are afraid, O Muhammad, go forward! You need not fear when you are in a state of *Īmān-Islām.* You have the grace of My protection, the only true protection. I am the only One who can protect you in this way. Those who keep Me as their Protector will never be destroyed by anything in the world, but those who do not seek My help will be destroyed. As long as they have the world within them, they will be destroyed by that world. It is the world which kills the world. That is certain. Tell this to your followers.

"The world does not belong to you, O Muhammad. You are here to realize Me. That is why I showed you My actions, and that is why I created all My creations and their secrets. They are all examples I gave you so that you could understand Me. I am the only One who can perform these duties of creating, protecting, nourishing, giving food, and dispensing judgment. No one else can perform these actions.

"O Muhammad, through Adam, through My creations, through the earth, the sky, the sun, the moon, the stars, fire, water, air, and the clouds, I have revealed My secrets. Then I sent you to teach your followers. Through you, I sent them so many words and holy verses, so many actions, and so much wisdom. I gave the verses of the Holy Qur'an into your hands so that you could understand the connection between Myself and true man[19] and through this connection understand your earnings in this world and the hereafter. The nature of your true wealth is explained in the Holy Qur'an.

---

18. Ḥabīb Ibn Mālik: A prince of the major Arabian tribes who was asked by Abū Jahl to question Muhammad in the hope of proving him a false prophet. According to some narratives, Muhammad performed several miracles including the splitting of the moon (referred to in the 54th chapter of the Qur'an), thus convincing Ḥabīb and converting him to Islam.
Abū Jahl: One of the foremost adversaries of Muhammad. His real name was 'Amr Ibn Misham but the Muslims nicknamed him Abū Jahl, or the "Father of Ignorance."

19. *insān*

"Muhammad, you have revealed My word. If your followers want to learn the glory of the Qur'an, if they want to understand its wealth, they must have the wisdom of divine knowledge. The Qur'an is the secret[20] within the secret, the essence[21] within the essence, wisdom within wisdom, grace within grace, the soul[22] within the soul, the heart within the innermost heart,[23] the light within the light of the eye, the ear within the ear, the nose within the nose, the tongue within the tongue, and knowledge within divine knowledge. The Qur'an is the form[24] that exists within the form. They must go within to know its real meaning.

"Tell your followers that anyone who is under My protection can never be destroyed, but anyone who leaves My protection and My help to wage holy war now will destroy himself. Tell them that if one man seeks to kill or overcome another man, it is his own brothers that he will be destroying. And they, in turn, will destroy him. Man has the choice of turning into a beast or becoming like his Lord.[25] He has the potential to become a true realized being. If he becomes Adam, then I will correct his faults and protect him, just as I protected Adam.

"Muhammad, tell this to your followers. They were all in darkness and torpor before they knew you. I made them come out of hiding and follow you, did I not? Earlier they were hidden in satan, but now they are your companions, your warriors. Who were they before? What were their actions earlier compared to their actions now? They were just like the people against whom they now want to wage war. Just like these children of Adam, they were hidden in the same darkness, entangled in the same desires and illusions and elemental miracles.[26] They too were buried within satan.

"But with My words, you led them out of the darkness, and they began to follow you and to follow Me, their Lord and Creator, did they not? Are they your enemies now? No, they have lost themselves and dedicated their lives to you and to Me. Abū Bakr,

20. *sirr*

21. *dhāt*

22. *rūḥ*

23. *qalb*

24. *ṣūrah*

25. *Rabb*

26. *siddhis*

'Umar Ibn Al-Khaṭṭāb, 'Uthmān, and Ḥamzah[27] were all hidden in darkness. Look how they emerged. Therefore, would it be right to destroy others who are in that darkness now?

"So, tell your followers, rather than waging holy war, they should try to bring such people out of the darkness and make them understand Allah. Instead of fighting against them, they should help them accept the truth, strengthen their faith, certitude, and determination, and try to change them.

"To convert without force is the way of Islam; to destroy and kill and slaughter people is not. Therefore, tell your followers that the holy war they must wage is one of lifting up those who have fallen into the state of disbelief.[28] Tell them to use My actions, My words, and My behavior in order to release those who are hidden in satan and buried in illusion. That is the true holy war. That is Islam. Reveal this to your followers."

In this way, Allah's commandments came to His Messenger to show his companions the ways of justice. Allah could have destroyed all the unbelievers, but instead He brought them forth from the darkness.

But not all of the followers of Muhammad were able to attain this compassionate state. Some did not have the strength of inner patience, contentment, and trust in God. They were not able to say, "If God wills," and "Whatever God wills."[29] And so they continued to plead, "Let us ruin those who are trying to ruin us. O Prophet, we are not like you, we are ordinary people just like they are. We have to fight force with force." The Prophet tried to teach them patience, but they had this need in their hearts.

Finally Allah gave His permission, "All right, tell them to begin

---

27. Abū Bakr al-Siddīq: The first caliph and a father-in-law to the Prophet.
'Umar Ibn al-Khaṭṭāb: The second caliph and a father-in-law to the Prophet. At first he was violently opposed to Muhammad, but later heard his sister reciting part of the Qur'an and was overcome. Going directly to Muhammad, he professed his belief in Allah and His Prophet. See also Chapter 3.
'Uthmān: The third caliph; compiled the verses of the Qur'an and produced the authorized version which is still in existence.
Ḥamzah: Paternal uncle and foster brother of the Prophet.

28. *kufr*

29. *in shā'a Allāh* and *mā shā'a Allāh*

their holy war." But as they were preparing for battle, certain restrictions were placed upon them. They were told, "Do not fight this war for the sake of your pride, to show that you are a warrior or that you are strong. Fight only against those who come to fight with you. You may engage in combat only with someone who has taken your possessions. You must not usurp the possessions of another. You must not touch their women or harm their children. You must not destroy their houses or their farms and crops or kill their livestock. You must not cut down their trees, destroy the countryside, or ruin their wells. You must not kill those who run away in fear, and you must not strike someone who falls down in battle. Only if someone comes at you with a sword in his hand may you defend yourself."

The Prophet conveyed these rules to 'Alī and to Abū Bakr al-Siddīq.[30] "Go and fight," he said, "but do not go beyond these limits. If you fail to obey these rules you will be great sinners. If you wage war with the intention of acquiring land, houses, possessions, or happiness, forgetting the rules that I have given, then you will be blamed and will have to answer on the Day of Questioning."[31] Allah established all these restrictions and then told Muhammad, "Tell them to go in this state and regain what is rightfully theirs."

This was the way in which holy war was waged during the time of the Prophet. But even so, Muhammad did not take part in these battles. Instead, he spent the entire time praying for the fighting to stop. He remained alone, hands outstretched, praying to Allah. Every second his heart was crying, and the light in his eyes was directed toward Allah.

"Change their hearts," he prayed. "O Allah, make them accept You. Make them praise You and pray to You. Give them that certitude and love. Fill them with Your love and grace. Give them unity. Let them drop the swords from their hands and raise the

---

30. 'Alī: The fourth caliph, son-in-law of the Prophet, husband of Fatimah, and father of Ḥasan and Ḥusayn. The second convert to Islam, following Khadijah, the first wife of the Prophet.
Abū Bakr al-Siddīq: A father-in-law of the Prophet and the first caliph.

31. *Qiyāmah*

sword of perfect faith." The only sword that ever touched the Prophet's hands was the sword of inner patience, contentment, trust in God, and praise of God, the sword of love and of the unity of brotherhood. We must think about this.

A Direct Revelation to 'Alī

One day when 'Alī was in battle, his opponent's sword broke and the man fell. 'Alī stood above him, and holding his sword to the man's chest, he said, "If you had a sword in your hand, I would continue this fight, but since your sword is broken, I cannot strike you."

"If I had a sword at this moment, I would cut off your arms and legs," the man shouted back.

"All right then," 'Alī replied, and he handed the man his sword.

"What are you doing?" the man asked, bewildered. "I am your enemy, am I not?"

'Alī looked him in the eye and said, "You swore that if you had a sword in your hand you would kill me. Now you have my sword, so go ahead and strike me." But the man could not. "That was your ignorance and arrogance speaking," 'Alī explained. "In the realm of Allah, there is no fight or enmity between you and me. We are brethren. The real war is between the truth and your lack of wisdom. It is between truth and falsehood. You and I are just watching that battle. You are my brother. If I were to harm you at this point, I would have to answer for it on the Day of Questioning. Allah would ask me about it."

"Is this the way of Islam?" the man asked.

"Yes," 'Alī replied. "These are the words of Allah, the All-Powerful, Unique One."

Immediately the man bowed down at 'Alī's feet and begged, "Teach me the *kalimah.*"[32]

And 'Alī taught him, "There is no god but God. Nothing exists other than You, O God."[33]

---

32. The affirmation of faith.

33. *Lā ilāh illā Allāh*

A similar thing happened during a later battle. 'Alī felled his opponent, placed his foot on the man's chest, and held a sword to his neck. But again he did not kill the man.

"Why don't you kill me?" the man shouted angrily. "I am your enemy. Why are you just standing there?" And he spit in 'Alī's face.

At first 'Alī became angry, but then he removed his foot from the man's chest and put aside his sword. "I am not your enemy," 'Alī replied. "The real enemies are the evil qualities within us. You are my brother, yet you spit in my face. When you spat upon me, I became angry, and the arrogance of the I came to me. If I had killed you when I was in that state, then I would be a sinner, a murderer. I would have become the very thing I was fighting against. That crime would be recorded against my name, and I would have to answer for it later, when Allah questions me. That is why I cannot slay you."

"Then is there no fight between you and me?" the man asked.

"No. The battle is between wisdom and ignorance, between truth and falsehood," 'Alī told him. "Even though you spat on me and taunted me to kill you, I cannot."

"Where did such a rule come from?"

"These are the rules of Allah. This is Islam." Immediately, the man fell before 'Alī's feet, and he too was taught the *kalimah.*

This is the difference between the ways of Allah and the ways of the world. People shout, "*Jihād!*" which means holy war, but there are two kinds of *jihād.* The real holy war is an inner war, and those who fight that war follow Allah's rules. But those who fight for the sake of wife, children, or house follow other rules. If even an atom's worth of such thoughts are present, it is not a true holy war, but rather, a political war. It is fought for the sake of land and country, not for the sake of Allah. With wisdom, we must understand what the true *jihād* is, and we must think about the answers we will have to give on the Day of Questioning.

Muhammad and his followers had certitude, unity, justice, and conscience. It was in this state that their holy war was waged and the battles of Badr and Uhud[34] were fought. Some people were killed, but after these battles peace reigned in Islam. The greeting of peace,[35] the glorification[36] of Allah and the Prophet, and the words, "*Allāh Akbar!* God is Most Great!" resonated throughout the land.

We must understand this. The Prophet returned to capture Mecca, not with the sword, but with Allah's praise. Mecca was conquered with *Īmān-Islām,* with love, compassion, unity, and faith, with inner patience, contentment, trust in God, and praise of God. It was through these qualities that Islam grew. It was Allah's qualities that conquered the people.

Whatever is conquered by the sword does not last. The one who picks up the sword will one day die by that same sword. The one who picks up a gun will die by the gun. Whatever one raises in enmity, that very same weapon will cause his destruction. Whatever trick a man learns will bring about his destruction one day.

However, the one who receives the complete wealth of Allah's love, compassion, faith, and certitude will have eternal life.[37] That beauty of Islam and that resplendence will not die in this world or in in the world of the souls.[38] Such a one will be different and his body will be different. Although his body belongs to the world, the qualities within him will belong to the hereafter. He will be like the lotus flower which lives in the water yet does not keep the water within itself. He will live in this world, but the world will not be within him. Only Allah's qualities and His beauty will exist there.

---

34. Badr: The battle of Badr was fought between the followers of Muhammad and those among the Quraysh who rejected the belief in Allah and Muhammad. Many of Islam's principle opponents were killed including Abū Jahl. The victory of Badr established the ability of the Muslims to defend themselves.

    Uhud: The battle of Uhud was also between the followers of Muhammad and the Quraysh. The outcome of the battle was mixed, the Muslims being outflanked by Khālid Ibn al-Walīd, a great warrior among the Quraysh who later embraced Islam. The Quraysh however did not pursue their advantage and were forced to retreat by the regrouped Muslims.

35. *salām*

36. *ṣalawāt*

37. *ḥayāh*

38. *'ālam al-arwāḥ*

Reflect upon this. There is nothing that the All-Powerful One cannot do. Shedding blood is not the way. Instead, we must cut away our arrogance, karma, and illusion. We must cut away this darkness of ignorance and establish light. This is the only way to spread wisdom and divine knowledge.

Do not shout, *"Allāh Akbar!* God is Most Great!" and then kill someone. Instead lead him to the good path, the straight path, and say, *"Allāh Akbar."* That is *Īmān-Islām.* True holy war means to kill the inner enemy, the enemy to truth. But instead people shout, *"Jihād!"* and go to kill an external enemy. That is not holy war. We should not spread Islam through the sword; we must spread it through the *kalimah,* through truth, faith, and love. We have to think about this.

If you believe in Allah, the Unique, All-Pervasive Power, then His peaceful state, His greetings of peace, His love, His compassion, His wisdom, His equality, His comfort, and His qualities will be your weapons. This is what was explained to the companions of the Prophet. It is with these weapons alone that we should make our holy war. These are the weapons of Allah, the All-Powerful, Unique One, the weapons of the state of oneness with God.[39]

Do we really need to wage war against others for His sake? Do we really need to destroy others with swords? No, it is not necessary for us to kill in this way. How can we accept the *kalimah* of the All-Powerful, Unique One if we do that? Instead, we need to discard what He has discarded. He is the Almighty One who can create and destroy within the blinking of an eye. Allah can do things before we even think of them. Life and death belong to Him, not to us.

If we think about it, we will see that there are many explanations in the words of Allah and the words of the Prophet. We must understand the knowledge within divine knowledge that exists in the traditions of the Prophet and the Qur'an. We cannot study only the surface meanings; we must dig deep to see what is within. For every issue, we must think, "What did the exalted Prophet say about this? What revelations have been given about this? What has

---

39. *tawḥīd*

been said about this to those with divine wisdom? What has been said to the companions of the Prophet, the ones with the clarity of wisdom? And what has been said to the ones without wisdom?" For each question there are many explanations that have been given. For each person's level of wisdom, an appropriate reply has been given. We need to understand the words of Allah that were sent to us. If we understand the inner meanings of those words it will be good. My love to you, my children.

Allah's holy war is a good thing. It is a battle against all the enemies within us. We must raise His weapons of love, compassion, mercy, comfort, patience, and contentment. Then we will have victory over everything. The weapons used in the outer battles are implements of destruction. Knives and swords can never bring victory; they can only destroy. Allah's weapons never destroy.

My love to you. Amen.

إِيْمَانٌ

Īmān

Absolute faith, certitude, and determination

Faith alone can capture another heart. Faith alone can rule the world. The qualities of Allah that exist within the heart of one with determined faith must reach out, enter the heart of another, and give him comfort and peace. It is Allah's qualities that can conquer people and nations.

THE SPREAD OF ISLAM

أَعُوذُ بِٱللَّهِ مِنَ ٱلشَّيْطَانِ ٱلرَّجِيمِ بِسْمِ ٱللَّهِ ٱلرَّحْمَٰنِ ٱلرَّحِيمِ

I seek refuge in Allah from the evils of the accursed satan.
In the name of Allah, Most Merciful, Most Compassionate.

May all the peace, the beneficence, and the blessings of God be upon you.[1]

My brothers and sisters in Islam who are true believers,[2] I give you my greetings. May the peace of Allah be upon you.[3]

It has been 1,408 years since the congregation called Islam emerged from among the children of Adam. Allah, all glory and exaltedness be His,[4] perfected the state of true Islam with the coming of the Final Prophet, Muhammad, His Chosen Messenger. Through the Angel Gabriel, Allah sent the Holy Qur'an as revelations to His Prophet. In turn, Muhammad explained the five principles of Islam[5] to the great holy men of divine wisdom,[6] to the saints, to the archangels, and to all mankind.

But Islam is not just 1,408 years old. Islam is truth. It is Allah's radiant light, His qualities and actions, His attributes, and His compassion. It is perfect purity. Allah placed this purity within man when He created Adam. Islam, therefore, existed even before the creation of man. It existed in the world of the pure souls.[7] This has been revealed in the traditional stories of Islam.[8]

Truth is one and Islam is one. It shows no preference for any

1. *al-salām 'alaykum wa-raḥmat Allāh wa-barakātuhu kulluh*
2. *mu'min*
3. *al-salām 'alaykum*
4. *subḥānahu wa-ta'ālá*
5. The five obligatory duties of Islam: faith, prayer, charity, fasting, and pilgrimage to Mecca.
6. *quṭbs*
7. *'ālam al-arwāḥ*
8. *aḥādīth*

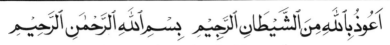

particular religion, sect, race, or tribe. It sees no differences between black, white, red, and yellow. It does not distinguish between people from China and people from Africa, America, Europe, Australia, Asia, Russia, or any country in the world. It does not even show differences between those in the realm of the primal beginning[9] and those in the hereafter.[10] The word Islam has only one meaning: the unity and peacefulness of truth. That truth is Allah. He rules all the universes with His truth and peacefulness and with absolute faith, certitude, and determination.[11] Islam is comprised of His three thousand gracious qualities and attributes, His unity, tranquility, and virtuous conduct, His equality, and His compassion. They are His wealth. To attain that wealth we recite the *kalimah,* "There is nothing other than You, O God. Only You are Allah."[12] God is the One to whom we pray. He is the truth which we must accept in this world and in the hereafter.

My brothers who are true believers must realize this. Islam must realize this. There should be no divisions among those who, with perfect faith, have accepted the truth of Allah and affirmed the *kalimah.* All those who worship Him and pray to Him should pray in unity. All must unite as one in times of sorrow and in times of joy, in death and in life. To be in Islam means to be united as one congregation in all three realms: in the primal beginning, in this world, and even in the hereafter. It means to see Him face to face, worshiping Him, and greeting Him with peace in our hearts.

Here and in the hereafter, we must embrace all those who with absolute faith accept Allah in their hearts. We must pray to Allah in a state of unity, peacefulness, and truth, and then give greetings of peace to each brother. Standing face to face, our eyes looking directly into our brother's eyes, our hands clasping his hands, and our hearts embracing his heart with love, we must say, "May the peace of God be upon you."

This is the unity and beauty of Islam, the beauty that Muhammad brought to the people. Wherever we go, our hearts must be in that state. Our prayers must be one-pointed, directed

9. *al-awwal*

10. *al-ākhirah*

11. *īmān*

12. *Lā ilāh illā Allāh*

toward the same place, toward Allah, the One who is truth. If we can recite the praises of Allah and the Prophet,[13] then look each other in the eye, give peaceful greetings, and embrace each other—if we can achieve that oneness of the heart with all lives, then we will be true believers.

As brothers in Islam, we must open our hearts and look within. Without jealousy, envy, deceit, or trickery, without divisiveness or discrimination, we must turn our hearts to the straight path and glorify Allah. Accepting the truth and abiding by it, we must establish that truth in the right manner, with love, forbearance, and equality. This is the state of *Īmān-Islām,* which the Prophet explained 1,408 years ago. This is what is spoken of in the Qur'an.

My brothers, before the time of Prophet Muhammad, there were many, many divisions and sects among the people of Mecca. They worshiped three hundred and sixty different idols, which they housed in the *Ka'bah.*[14] They performed mantras, magics, and miracles. Although so many prophets had come to the world, including Adam, Noah, Abraham, Ishmael, Moses, and many others, Mecca was still a place of idol worship. Those who lived at this time are commonly referred to as the ignorant ones.[15] Even after Muhammad came and taught the *kalimah,* most of the people in both Mecca and Medina still had no faith and rejected his teachings. They were referred to as unbelievers.[16]

But did Islam reject the people of Mecca and Medina? No. It was not the purpose of the Prophet to divide or to create enmity. Islam tells us not to discard the unbelievers or those who are ignorant, but rather to transform them. Once they acquire faith and their hearts are filled with light, once they perform their prayers to Allah alone, they too will be in Islam.

All those in Islam must reflect on this today. If we consider the way in which the Prophet transformed the people of Mecca and Medina, can we not follow that same process now, in the rest of the

13. *ṣalawāt*

14. The cube-like building in the center of the mosque in Mecca.

15. *jāhils*

16. *kāfirs*

world? Islam is compassion, tolerance, forbearance, and the gracious qualities of Allah. It should not create barriers or divide people; it should show them the way and invite them into itself. That was the way of Muhammad and the way of the earlier prophets.

Just as the Prophet transformed the unbelievers into Islam through his love and his gracious qualities, each one of you must turn those evil qualities within yourself into good qualities. You must develop inner patience, contentment, trust in Allah, and praise of Allah.[17] Only then can you truly be a follower of Islam.

It is these good qualities and good thoughts that can attract and capture the hearts of others. It is love that can open and reveal a person's innermost heart to himself. Once his heart is opened, absolute faith can bring him to a state of steadfastness. Then that person is ready to go in search of the truth, and when he finds the truth, he will find Allah, who is that truth. And once he finds the justice and the peacefulness of Allah, he too will be able to dispense justice and peacefulness throughout the world. In this state, he will glorify Allah, the Protector, the Most Compassionate. Such a man will embrace and comfort others with his life, his heart, and his body. This is how the individual, the world, and Allah's kingdom of justice can be ruled by the qualities which emerge from within the heart of one who has absolute faith, certitude, and determination.

You should not call anyone an unbeliever. When your love goes out and embraces the hearts of others, when truth enters their hearts and perfect faith conquers them, at that moment, at the very instant that faith appears in their hearts, they are in Islam, are they not? They have turned around and hoisted the flag of Islam, have they not? At that moment, those whom you once called unbelievers are changed. They accept Allah as the truth and now they worship only Him. Only the grace called faith can overcome and conquer the unbelievers.

Faith alone can capture another heart. Faith alone can rule the world. The qualities of Allah that exist within the heart of one with determined faith must reach out, enter the heart of another, and

---

17. *ṣabr, shukr, tawakkul 'alá Allāh,* and *al-ḥamdu lillāh*

give him comfort and peace. It is seeing Allah's compassion, His equality, His tranquility, His integrity, His honesty, and the manner in which He embraces and protects all lives with equal justice which can bring a person to the state of harmony and compel him to bow in unity. It is these qualities that can conquer people and nations. They begin by capturing the hearts of a few, then they reach out to all those in the village, then the city, and eventually these qualities reach out to the entire population of the country.

Through Allah, faith can conquer the primal beginning, this world, the hereafter,[18] and all of everything. This is the proof that Allah alone rules His kingdom. This is how true Islam spreads, not by going to war to conquer other lands. If we can complete the war within ourselves against our own bad qualities, then our faith will be able to conquer other hearts and other countries.

To be in Islam is to act with virtue, modesty, compassion, peacefulness, forbearance, Allah's three thousand gracious attributes, His unity, His tranquility, and His equality. Islam embraces all equally in both joy and sorrow. If one is hungry, all are hungry. If one is sad, all are sad. If one is happy, all are happy.

In this state of Islam, if we have a quarrel with somebody after the afternoon prayer,[19] we must make peace, and embrace each other by the time of the early evening prayer.[20] Any evil influences created must be thrown away before the next time of prayer. We must ask God for forgiveness for the faults we committed and strive for repentance. For what is happening now, during this very breath, we must glorify His name. And we must surrender to God the next breath, the next time of prayer to come. Whether or not we are alive in the next moment is Allah's will. May His will be fulfilled. If we have this faith with perfect certitude, if we have this intention with every breath, if we can acquire His qualities and His actions, then that is the state of Islam lived by true believers.

Whatever suffering each one of us faces, we must have patience.

---

18. *al-awwal, dunyā,* and *al-ākhirah*

19. *'aṣr*

20. *maghrib*

If we undergo even greater suffering, we must have contentment. If we undergo still greater difficulty we must surrender it to God. And when our suffering extends yet further, beyond our endurance, we can do nothing but praise Him. This is Islam—to praise Allah for whatever happens.

To worry about what has happened before or what is to come later is not Islam. If one constantly worries about what has gone by, his heart will be filled with grief and darkness. Grief and darkness are not Islam. Envy, jealousy, and treachery are not Islam. For what has gone by, all we can do is ask for forgiveness and strive for repentance,[21] and then complete whatever needs to be done now. This is the correct state of Islam, the state that a man who is a true believer must attain.

If our hearts attain this state of clarity, we will never see differences anywhere. If His qualities develop in us, we will never show discrimination toward anyone. Allah does not see any differences. Truth sees no differences. The prayer that accepts Allah as the only One worthy of worship sees no divisions. His equality and His peacefulness do not see any differences. Islam brings that equality and that peacefulness to every heart. It demonstrates unity and compassion to every heart.

Just getting together and talking about these things is not the true voice of Islam. Islam is not idle talk. In order to give voice to Islam, we must bring these words into our hearts, make them steadfast within us, and then act accordingly. We must praise Allah saying, "All praise is to You,"[22] greet His prophets, saying, "God bless them and grant them peace,"[23] and greet those who have faith, saying, "May the peace of God be upon you." That is the true voice of Islam. Coming together to glorify Allah alone is Islam.

We must bring God's qualities into action within us. This is the command of Allah, shown to us by every prophet He sent, from Adam to Prophet Muhammad. If every one of us can establish this

21. *tawbah*

22. *al-ḥamdu lillāh*

23. The *ṣalawāt: Sallá Allāh 'alayhim wa-sallam.*

state, if we can exhibit and prove this within our own hearts, we will be true believers. May we who have the determined faith of true believers think deeply about this. May every heart reflect on this. The kings who are true believers, the elders who are true believers, the rulers, the learned ones, the teachers, and those with the wealth of Allah[24]—all those who are true believers—must reflect upon this. Our entire generation must reflect upon this.

We must understand the words of Allah, the words of the Prophet, and the treasure of grace buried within the Qur'an. We must embrace that treasure to our own hearts before we can explain it to the hearts of others and help them to accept it. The Qur'an is our treasury, the wealth of Islam, from which everything comes. Even though we may be poor in this world, we can earn the wealth of God in the hereafter. The wealth of this world will be left behind, but the wealth of His qualities, His actions, and the divine knowledge[25] of His grace[26] will be with us forever. Those who have made their hearts the repository of this wealth of Allah's grace and have acquired that divine knowledge and put it into practice are the ones who can truly be called the wealthy ones in the hereafter.

May this beneficence which Allah has given fill the hearts of everyone around us, in all three realms of the primal beginning, this world, and the hereafter. May their hearts be filled with the wealth of grace-awakened wisdom,[27] the wealth of prayer and worship,[28] and the wealth of justice. And may we make our hearts the repository of Allah's wealth and share it with the hearts of our brothers and sisters. May we strive hard to help them fill their hearts with divine knowledge and faith, so that they will be the wealthy ones in the hereafter. May all attain peace within their hearts. May we make every effort to do this. In our prayer, in our congregations, in the mosques, in our jobs, in our worldly life, in death and in life, in sorrow and in joy—may we strive for only this wealth, this unity, this grace.

My very precious brothers who have opened out the umbrella of

---

24. *dawlah*

25. *'ilm*

26. *raḥmah*

27. *gnānam*

28. *'ibādah*

grace called Islam, unfurled the flag of perfect faith, and walked on the good path, with awareness in our hearts, let us establish this state of unity called Islam and lead our lives in that unity. Amen.

Certain words may have been repeated here, but they contain meanings which must be said over and over and over again until they are understood. They have been repeated so that we will gain more and more understanding each time we read them. Therefore, please forgive the repetition. Please forgive us in the name of Allah and Muhammad. These are the words that came to our heart. Please do not reject them.

If there is any fault, please forgive me in the name of Allah and His Messenger. I give peaceful greetings to all of you.

May all the peace, the beneficence, and the blessings of God be upon you. Amen. May Allah guide us on the path of equality and peacefulness. May He strengthen our faith, take us on the straight path, and accept us. Amen.

PART THREE: UNITY

Ittihād

Unity

We must make all people one with us. The Prophet Muhammad explained this to us, but some of us who came to the world forgot the message Allah sent. We must learn to wash away our separations and become one again. That is true Islam.

UNITY: THE SECRET OF CREATION

أَعُوذُ بِاللَّهِ مِنَ الشَّيْطَانِ الرَّجِيمِ بِسْمِ اللَّهِ الرَّحْمَٰنِ الرَّحِيمِ

I seek refuge in Allah from the evils of the accursed satan.
In the name of Allah, Most Merciful, Most Compassionate.

To Allah alone belongs the responsibility for the beginning and the end of all things. He alone knows the secrets of all the creations of the eighteen thousand universes. May we praise only Him. Amen.

In this world, Allah created many different kinds of beautiful and valuable things, but there would have been no creation at all if the five elements had not come together in unity. Earth, fire, water, air, and ether are natural enemies to one another, but God joined them together through the recitation of the *kalimah:* "There is no god except the one God, and Muhammad is His Messenger."[1] It was through the light of *Nūr Muḥammad,*[2] that He united them, saying, "O Muhammad, without you I would not have created anything. I have created everything through you."

Before the five elements joined together as one, each proclaimed with great pride, "I! I! There is no one greater than I! I can do anything I want." Water said, "I can do anything I want." Air said, "I can do anything I want." Earth and fire and ether also said, "I can do anything I want." Each one boasted that it was invincible. But if we consider everything that was created out of these five energies, we will see that they all contain some imperfection or weakness[3] and that they all are subject to change and destruction. Except for the All-knowing and Almighty Eternal God, everything is

1. *Lā ilāh illā Allāh Muḥammad Rasūl Allāh*

2. The light which became completeness within Allah and then emerged.

3. *ḥayf*

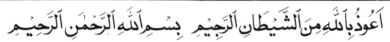

imperfect and will change.

To break the pride of the five elements, to destroy their arrogance, and to bring them together in unity, God showed them their many weaknesses.

To earth He said, "Do not think that you are great. Good and evil and all that is filthy and discarded exist within you. And everyone steps on you."

"I am indeed full of faults," the earth was forced to admit.

"Recite the *kalimah* in the name of the light of *Nūr Muḥammad,*" God commanded. And earth recited the *kalimah.*

Then God told water, "You wash away dirt from others, but then you keep it all within yourself, and the millions of worms and insects and germs that grow within you make you smell terrible. What is more, you have no shape of your own; you are trapped by what surrounds you. Only when there is an opening can you flow out and escape. O water, how can you say that you are great, when you can be pushed about by winds and blocked by earth from going wherever you want?"

"I certainly have many faults," admitted water.

"Recite the *kalimah* in the name of the light of *Nūr Muḥammad,*" God commanded. And water recited the *kalimah.*

Then God told fire, "You think you can do whatever you want, but air can blow you out and water can drown you. That should put an end to your arrogance. There is only One who is without fault. That One is Allah, the eternal One who has no beginning or end."

And fire also had to admit, "I am full of faults."

"Recite the *kalimah* in the name of the light of *Nūr Muḥammad,*" commanded God. And fire recited the *kalimah.*

Next God told air, "You look at everyone's face, but no one looks at your face. You think you are great, but there are tall mountain ranges that can block you. And when houses, trees, or mountains stand in your way, what can you do? Nothing."

"I have many faults," admitted air.

"Then recite the *kalimah* and know that there is someone greater than you. That One is Allah." And air recited the *kalimah.*

Then God told ether, "You are maya, you are illusion. You are nothing but glitters. One storm pushes you this way, the next pushes you that way. As soon as daylight comes, your glitters disappear and the beauty of your own light fades. You are powerless in the daylight."

"I am full of faults," admitted ether.

"Recite the *kalimah,*" God commanded. And ether recited the sacred words.

And so, when the five acknowledged their deficiencies, affirmed their faith,[4] and said the *kalimah* in the name of the light of *Nūr Muḥammad,* they became one, and Islam came into being. Only after they recited the *kalimah* did they join together in unity.

That unity found within all creation is Islam. For both the beginning and the end, Islam came in the form of unity. It came through Prophet Muhammad, through *Nūr Muḥammad,* through *Aḥmad,* through the Muhammad of the nine meanings.[5] When Allah said, "O Muhammad, without you I would not have created anything, then or now," He was speaking about that light of Muhammad which has existed as Islam since the beginning, in the world of the souls,[6] and which will exist forever. He was not referring to something that came with the Prophet Muhammad 1408 years ago. If Islam only began on that date, then what happened to all the prophets and all the people who came before that?

In the time of Adam, people worshiped many deities. Were they sent to hell? Did God send Adam to hell? So many yugas and eons have passed since then, so many people have come and gone. Did they all go to hell? No, those who understood and attained clarity in the past were certainly within Islam. They were true believers,[7] and

---

4. *īmān*

5. The nine meanings refer to nine names of Muhammad: *Anāthi Muḥammad* (The Unmanifested); *Āthi Muḥammad* (The Manifested); *Awwal Muḥammad* (The Beginning, the emergence of creation); *Ḥayāh Muḥammad* (The *Rūḥ,* the emergence of the soul); *An'um Muḥammad* (The *Rizq,* the food or nourishment, for all creations); *Aḥmad* (The *Qalb,* the innermost heart); *Muḥammad* (The Beauty in the face, a reflection of the beauty in the heart); *Nūr Muḥammad* (The Plenitude, the Light which became completeness within Allah and emerged); *Allāh Muḥammad* (The Light of Allah within *Muḥammad,* and the Light of *Muḥammad* within Allah).

6. *'ālam al-arwāḥ*

7. *mu'min*

they reached the eighth heaven.[8] The light of Muhammad existed as Islam in the beginning as it will in the end. God has been teaching the people step by step, sending the prophets one after another, each with a message for man, each with revelations for a particular time.

God has said that man is the most exalted among His creations, because he has divine analytic wisdom. If he becomes a true believer, he can know and see things that the heavenly beings cannot. God gave the jinns and fairies only thirty-six powers, but to man He has given ninety-six. Beyond those ninety-six powers are four more: true man,[9] Muhammad, *Nūr,*[10] and Allah. The state of a true man, the true form of Adam,[11] comes into being once wisdom resplends. Then, when the heart becomes radiant and shines in the face (*muham*) as the beauty of that face, that is the state of Muhammad. And when the light of wisdom becomes complete and ever present, that is the beauty of the *Nūr,* the effulgence of Muhammad. Finally, when we block off everything else and stand in silence as the *alif,*[12] and then raise our hands in praise of God,[13] that is Allah, resplending as wisdom, the One who makes silent things speak and makes them become visible within.

True man, Muhammad, *Nūr,* and Allah: these four, together with the ninety-six powers, represent the one hundred names of God.[14] God gave all but one of these names to man so that he could bring them into action. That one name, Allah, He kept for Himself. He is the One who never diminishes, the One who cannot be compared to anything. Allah is not like anything else. We can cut a rough stone, wash it, facet it, and compare its value with that of other stones, but Allah cannot be compared with any of His creations. He is without price, without comparison. He is the most valuable treasure of all, the treasure concealed within man. A man

---

8. *firdaws*
9. *insān*
10. The resplendence of Allah, the plenitude of the light of Allah.
11. *ṣūrat al-Ādam*
12. The first letter of the Arabic alphabet (ا) which to the transformed man represents Allah.
13. *takbīr*
14. *Asmā' al-ḥusná*

could not even move if Allah were not within him. And a true man is within Allah, hidden within Him, surrendered to Him. He keeps Allah within himself and Allah keeps that man within Him.

Allah created everything in unity. He created truth and the light of truth. He also created flower gardens with different kinds of flowers and countless precious gems with different kinds of light. And He created Adam, without whom no human beings would exist. Eve came from Adam, and they joined together and had twenty-one sets of twins. But instead of living together in unity, the children separated from each other and scattered throughout the land. As they settled in their different environments, they began to imitate the voices of the birds, animals, and other sounds there, and thus formed separate languages. As centuries passed, mankind developed more and more differences and forgot the meaning of Islam.

Allah made all of His creations as one, but some of them have separated and become soiled. Some who came in the form of men behave like animals, while some who came in the form of animals behave like men. An animal or even a satan can be like a man, and a man can be like an animal or a satan. Even though there are such things as evil beings, that does not mean we should discard them, saying, "They do this, they do that. They are not like us. They must be kept separate." Instead we must wash away the dirt and become one again. If a man's shirt gets splashed with mud, does that make it a different shirt? We cannot say that. He doesn't throw it out and say, "This shirt has changed. It is different." It is the same shirt that he bought, and if he washes it, it will return to its original state.

Similarly, you don't discard someone because he falls. You should wash him with the *kalimah,* with wisdom and absolute faith, with unity and good qualities. And when the time comes, he will learn to clean himself. What can we show him in the meantime? Love. Our love must be like soap. If we show the qualities of compassion, love, charity, generosity, justice, and peace, that will bring him along.

We are not Muslims if we discard someone saying, "He holds another belief. He belongs to a different religion. His color is not like ours." None of that matters; what we need is to be one. The only real difference between men lies in their conduct and actions, their qualities, and their faith, certitude, and determination. When these are correct, then men are one, with no differences. So, we must keep the good things and wash away the dirt. We must wash our innermost hearts[15] until they become light. We must make all people one with us. The Prophet Muhammad explained this to us, but some of us who came to the world forgot the message Allah sent. We must learn to wash away our separations and become one again. That is true Islam. True Islam has never discarded anyone. Once we entrust the *kalimah* to Allah, we will never again perceive anyone as different from us. We will begin to love our neighbors as ourselves.

We must stop looking at the outside, at colors and other such things. If you peel off the skin of a dog, its flesh will look the same as that of a deer. If you peel off the skin of a pig, its flesh might look like that of a goat. You may not even be able to tell the difference between the flesh of an animal and the flesh of a child. All flesh is the same color, only the skin looks different. No matter what color a lampshade is, the light will still shine through. Light is always light. Truth and good qualities are the light in our hearts, and that light must shine within.

We have to look beyond what we see on the outside. A person may have strayed from the path or may follow some other religion, but he is still our neighbor. We must not discard anyone, no matter what belief he holds. We have to understand that people worship in many ways. Hindus may call themselves *saivam,* which means purity. Buddhists acknowledge purity. And Muslims say that Islam is purity. There are many different names for purity.

We must not scorn others just because they follow a different belief or speak a different language. People who know Arabic claim that Arabic is the highest language. Those who know Urdu say that Urdu is the greatest, Hindus claim that Hindi is the best, Tamil people say that Tamil is unequaled, and Buddhists say that Pali is the finest language. The English boast that English is spoken throughout the world; the Italians say that Latin is the language of

---

15. *qalb*

the scriptures; the Greeks say that Greek is superior; the Japanese and Chinese make the same claim. There are so many different languages, and yet each person claims superiority because of the language he speaks. But greatness does not come from words.

Words are just sounds. In one language a word may have a very nice meaning, but in another language it may be obscene. Often words can cause misunderstandings that lead to fights and disagreements.

Meaning does not lie in words themselves. It lies in understanding. There are so many meanings hidden within everything. There are things beyond, far beyond what we have studied up until now. We must understand this. A person who has learned several languages might think that he is very exalted, but he cannot speak the language that God has given to a bird! There is a story about a man who learned so much from a tiny bird that he threw away all his books.

> Once there was a very learned man named Imām al-Ghazzāli, who had written nine hundred and ninety-nine volumes about God. As he was finishing his one thousandth volume he began to think, "I have written everything there is to say. There is nothing beyond this."
>
> One day he came to the bank of a river near the city of Rum. After unloading his books from his camel, he cooked and bathed and then sat down to write the closing words of the final volume. Suddenly he saw a small bird, the size of a hummingbird, diving into the river. It flew to the tree under which Imām al-Ghazzāli was writing, perched itself on a twig, and dropped two drops of water from its tiny beak onto his book. Then it went back to the river, plunged into the water, flew back to its perch, and again dropped two more drops of water onto the book.
>
> Imām al-Ghazzāli knew the language of birds and so he asked, "O bird, what are you doing?"
>
> The bird replied, "I am emptying the river."
>
> Astonished, Imām al-Ghazzāli said, "Do you intend to drain the entire river? Why, you can carry only one or two

drops of water at a time. At this rate, how can you ever hope to drain the entire river?"

"Of course I can," the bird answered. "And I certainly will."

"But how can you possibly do that?" Imām al-Ghazzāli asked.

"Well," the little bird told him, "you have been claiming that you have reached the end of everything which can be written about Allah. If you can reach the end of describing Allah and His glory in a thousand books, surely I can drain this river!"

"This small bird has shown me the truth," Imām al-Ghazzāli thought. "I have wasted all this time carrying around a mound of books that amount to only a drop of knowledge, thinking that it was the entire river. These books are useless and must be thrown away."

And so all the one thousand books went into the river. Then the little bird said to him, "If you cannot write everything about Allah, then I certainly cannot drain the river. Therefore, I will go on my way. May the peace and peacefulness of God be upon you."

"And may the peace and peacefulness of God be upon you also,"[16] Imām al-Ghazzāli replied.

Three or four of those books were saved and are now circulating in the world as the works of Imām al-Ghazzāli. Out of the thousand books he wrote, only those few remain.

Now the bird in this story was really the Angel Gabriel. He came to Imām al-Ghazzāli to teach him wisdom, and he can also come in different forms to teach us. He may appear as a bird or as the wind, or even as a formless voice, or in the sounds of a child that cannot speak yet.

There are so many things we have to learn, so many hidden

16. *al-salām 'alaykum; wa 'alaykum al-salām.* A loving, respectful greeting and response.

meanings within things. But it is not enough just to read books. The clarity and understanding we must attain does not come from books; it is not something we can read about. To understand this we have to go beyond words, into our hearts; that is where He has revealed everything. We must dwell within Him and find the tongue that will reveal Him. If we have pride and say, "I have already learned so much. I am indeed learned," then nothing will be revealed to us. We can only attain wisdom if we grab hold of God and hold on and hold on, saying, "I surrender, I surrender, I surrender."

As soon as we accept this with absolute faith and go on the straight path to God, we will realize that the good and evil[17] in the world are within the responsibility of Allah.[18] We will reject the body, the world, and all that is evil, and accept all that is good and eternal. Then when suffering comes closer and closer to us, we will embrace Allah even more. And if we live in God's embrace rather than holding on to the world, everything will be revealed to us. But instead, when we suffer we tend to embrace the world in the way that a crab, when thrown into a fire, embraces the flames with its claws until it too becomes the fire. This is the way man behaves in his ignorance.

We have to embrace that one God who is without form. That is the highest point of the *kalimah.* Everything but Allah can be destroyed; only that Formless One is indestructible. We must prostrate before Allah as His slaves[19] and worship Him alone in the way that earth, fire, water, air, and ether did. We must accept our weaknesses, saying, "I am full of faults." Allah's beautiful qualities must come to bloom within our hearts, and that fragrance must emit a state of peace that will console and comfort all hearts.

My brothers and sisters, why do we all gather together in one place when we pray? For unity. Why do we all bow our heads at the same time? For unity. Everywhere in the world, Muslims bow their

17. *khayr* and *sharr*

18. *tawakkul 'alá Allāh*

19. *'abd*

heads as one. When we stand up, we stand up as one. When we bend, we bend together. When we all drop to the ground in prostration at the same time, it is like saying, "We are all dead!" And when we rise as one, that is like saying, "Come to life!" When we gather together in a Muslim house for a happy or sad occasion, we are as one. When we attend a funeral, we recite the funeral prayer in unison to show respect for a departed brother. In the name of God, we pay our respects before the corpse is buried. We do all these things in unity, because Islam is unity. In *Īmān-Islām,*[20] we must not discard anyone. We must discard only what is opposite to Allah, only what Allah has discarded.

Therefore, don't carry a sword, carry God's qualities. Don't carry a knife or a cannon, carry a heart of truth filled with God's beauty. Bear a compassionate face, radiant with the three thousand beautiful qualities of God. That will bring peace to others. That is Islam. Nothing in the world can conquer a heart with such qualities. Anything that tries to destroy such a heart will fail and be destroyed itself. Anything that tries to swallow something good will itself die.

We must reflect on this. We need to know how to conduct ourselves. We have to make ourselves into these qualities in order to realize our true worth. The taste of the fruit reveals the value of the tree. The fragrance and beauty of a flower show its value. The gleam from a polished gem demonstrates its worth. And we must use our lifetime to try to make ourselves valuable, to make ourselves perfectly clear. That is Islam. We can wear white clothes, but they will be white only as long as we keep them clean. How clean or dirty we are will show on our clothes. In the same way, what we think in our hearts, all the good and evil, is clearly visible to others. What is inside can be seen on the outside.

We must put an end to our desires and our connection to this world in order to know Islam. If we can shut out all that is evil we will see the good, but if we continue to shut out what is good, we will see only evil. We cannot see both at the same time.

---

20. *Īmān:* absolute faith, certitude, and determination.
Islām: the state of absolute purity.
See glossary.

It is like a mirror. In order to see the reflected light on one side of the glass, we must block the other side by covering it with silver. Similarly, in order to see the light of the hereafter[21] in the mirror of the heart, we must block off the world.[22] But we have to remember that whenever we try to block evil things, we will always meet with difficulties. Any time we try to dig for something good, we will experience a great deal of evil.

Anything we look at will have a dark side and a light side. When the sun shines on one side of the earth, the other side is in darkness. One side is revealed, the other side is hidden. The mind always wants to look at the dark side, at this world. If we look with the mind, the whole world will manifest itself and appear before us. That is how it takes form. However, to look at ourselves we must look into the light side of the mirror. If we look with clear faith and certitude into wisdom and God's qualities, we will see our own true image.

We have the form of man, and the light within us is a reflection which radiates from Allah. That radiance is Islam. But we are only able to see that light as a reflected image. The complete radiance of Islam extends from the time of creation to the hereafter. Allah alone is true Islam. We must always remember that from Allah we came to Adam as the light of the *Nūr*. We are all children of Adam. When we were created, we were adorned with many colors and given different sounds and voices. Just as each string on a stringed instrument produces a different sound, depending upon how the musician positions his fingers, the five strings of earth, fire, water, air, and ether that God placed within us will bring forth the right resonance when they are tuned and pressed in a certain way. In unity, those five strings will play, "There is no god other than the one God, and Muhammad is His Messenger. I witness that none is god except God; He is One without partner, and I witness that Muhammad is His slave and His Messenger."[23] That sound has the power to call

---

21. *al-ākhirah*

22. *dunyā*

23. The first *kalimah* and the *al-shahādah kalimah: Lā ilāh illā Allāh Muḥammad Rasūl Allāh. Ashhadu an lā ilāh illā Allāh waḥdahu lā sharīk lahu, wa-ashhadu anna Muḥammad 'abduhu wa rasūluh.* See appendix.

God. If our prayer, our remembrance,[24] our meditations and worship are established in that way, they too will reach God.

This is an important introduction to the teachings of Islam, the clear teachings brought by Prophet Muhammad, the teachings of the love of Allah. We must gently enter into this. We must study and learn. There are more than four hundred trillion, ten thousand evil spiritual forces we have to contend with. But goodness is one—Allah. May the unity and peacefulness of God be with you. Amen.

---

24. *dhikr*

أَشْهَدُ أَنْ لَا إِلٰهَ إِلَّا ٱللّٰهُ

وَحْدَهُ لَا شَرِيكَ لَهُ

وَأَشْهَدُ أَنَّ مُحَمَّدًا عَبْدُهُ وَرَسُولُهُ

The al-shahādah kalimah

Affirmation of faith

Ashhadu an lā ilāh illā Allāh waḥdahu lā sharīk lahu, wa-ashhadu anna Muḥammad ʻabduhu wa-rasūluh: I testify that none is god except God alone; He has no equal. And I testify that Muhammad is His servant and His Messenger.

Even if a rose has fifty petals, each one contains the same fragrance. Similarly, even if there are many millions of children in Islam, the beautiful fragrance of Allah's kalimah *will emanate from every one of them. It will be in their words, their thoughts, their actions, their devotion, and in their deep concentration on God.*

THE AFFIRMATION OF FAITH

أَعُوذُ بِٱللَّهِ مِنَ ٱلشَّيْطَانِ ٱلرَّجِيمِ بِسْمِ ٱللَّهِ ٱلرَّحْمَٰنِ ٱلرَّحِيمِ

I seek refuge in Allah from the evils of the accursed satan.
In the name of Allah, Most Merciful, Most Compassionate.

Allah is Most Great: *Allāh Akbar.* We are the people who have accepted Allah; we believe in the one God and follow His Messenger, Prophet Muhammad, who brought us the holy words of the second *kalimah:* I testify that none is god except God alone, He has no equal; and I testify that Muhammad is His servant and His Messenger.

Let us reflect upon this *kalimah* sent down by Allah to the Prophet. For whom are these words meant? Muhammad was born in Mecca into the Quraysh tribe. Does that mean that the *kalimah* is meant only for the Quraysh? No, it has spread to all the different tribes throughout Africa and the Middle East and to people the world over, of every race and religion. Look how many Muslims there are in the world today.

Who has the right to call himself a Muslim and who does not? To whom does Islam belong? Does it belong to one sect more than to another? A person might say he follows one of the four *imāms:* Imām Abū Ḥanīfah, Imām Mālik, Imām Ibn Ḥanbal, or Imām al-Shāfi'ī, but does it really matter to which family or tribe or sect

1. The *al-shahādah kalimah.* See appendix.
2. *Quraysh:* The Arabian tribe from which Muhammad was descended and of which his grandfather, 'Abd al-Muṭṭalib, was chief.
3. The four imāms: Imām Abū Ḥanifah: Born in al-Kufah A.H. 80 and died in Baghdad A.H. 150. Imām Mālik: Born and died in Medina A.H.94 - A.H.179. Imām Ibn Ḥanbal: Born and died in Baghdad A.H.164 - A.H.241. Imām āl-Shafi'ī: Born in Askalon, Pakistan A.H.150 and died in Cairo A.H.204.

continues on page 114

he belongs, or whether he is an Arab or not?

Allah belongs equally to everyone. Every tongue that has recited the *kalimah* with certitude belongs to the same family and dwells within Islam. They all bear witness to the oneness of Allah and to His Chosen Messenger,[4] Muhammad, the Final Prophet, the Prophet for the beginning and for the end; everything that was given in the beginning was made complete in him. All those who accept this truth and the one treasure called Allah are part of the same body of true believers.[5] They are all children born to one mother. To believe in Islam with perfect faith[6] is to live in that one body in unity.

Therefore, anyone who has truly accepted Prophet Muhammad and has faith in the *kalimah* will never harm or kill another who has also affirmed these words, no matter what fault that person may have committed. A tongue that has recited the *kalimah,* a tongue that has accepted Allah and His Messenger, should never attack another person in any way.

By affirming the *kalimah,* it is possible for us to attain a certain state, but we must remember that those who have not accepted it are still our neighbors. We must love them, not destroy them. Neighbors are not there to fight with, they are not there to be our enemies. Once we have recited the *kalimah,* we must show our neighbors only love, trust, and friendship. We must melt their hearts and make them trust us and embrace us. Then they will begin to act in the same way themselves.

Islam does not mean killing or attacking others. When such a thing happens, Islam is harming itself. To embrace others with love and to dispel their hunger, disease, poverty, and difficulties is Islam. To speak to someone from within the embrace of unity is Islam. To be together, to eat together, to live as one life in a state of affection is Islam. That is love, God's love, and Islam is the affection

---

These four men systematically developed the rules of conduct and law [*fiqh*] from the injunctions of the Qur'an and the *aḥādīth.* Four different schools of thought were established after them and each has a slightly different interpretation of the practices of Islam.

4. *Muṣṭafā al-Rasūl*

5. *mu'min*

6. *īmān*

displayed through that love. Islam is the compassion shown by acting with God's three thousand gracious qualities. Islam is establishing the praise of God and establishing the qualities of patience, contentment, surrendering all responsibility to God, and praising God for whatever happens.[7] One who is truly in Islam will practice these good qualities and continually beg of God, "O Allah, forgive all our faults and correct us."[8] That is what it means to be a true believer.

To become one is Islam. Just as the five fingers come together to form one hand, there is one group formed of all those who love Allah. In this world there are seventy-three different groups of human beings, and out of those, there is one group composed of all who have faith in God without the slightest doubt or wavering. That group is in true Islam.

For a Muslim there is only one race; there is no black, white, or yellow. There is no fighting and no division. How can we divide Islam and fight over it? How can we listen to people who goad us into conflict by complaining, "Those people are different from us"? The nature of true Islam is to bring together what has been divided. Once we were separate and scattered in many different directions, but the *kalimah* and Islam brought us together to worship the one God and embrace each other heart to heart.

True Islam is unity. We must be one. We must not create divisions by talk of different groups or different status. There are no divisions within Islam. Once someone has said the *kalimah* there is only one way to describe him: a child of Islam, nothing else. Earlier he might have been different, but now he is a Muslim. He might have followed another religion before, but as soon as he embraces the one God, he is in Islam.

Islam is *Allāh Akbar,* praising the one God as the Most Great. There are no titles or differences in Islam. There is only one great title: *Al-Mawlá,* the Lord, the Protector. We may call men of wisdom by the title of master, or *mawlāwi,* and we may even call those who have converted to Islam *mawlá al-Islām,* or friends of Islam, but

---

7. *ṣabr, shukr, tawakkul 'alá Allāh,* and *al-ḥamdu lillāh*

8. *astaghfiru Allāh al-'Aẓīm*

Allah alone is the Lord and Master of Islam, the only One worthy of worship. We are slaves to Him alone.

We must not create divisions in Islam by calling some high and others low. There is no such thing in the *kalimah.* Can we recite the *kalimah* and then separate Muslims into different categories, saying some are high and some are low? No, we cannot say that. A tree may have many branches, but the flowers and fruits on that tree are all the same. Is that not so? What does it matter if a fruit is on a lower branch or a higher one? Their seeds are the same.

We cannot show favoritism in Islam. We are all the creations of Allah, the children of Adam. the tribe of Abraham, the followers of Muhammad. Allah sends food to all and protects us all. And tomorrow He will question us all, no matter who we are or what position we hold. On the Day of Questioning[9] and the Day of Judgment, each of us will be judged for whatever good and evil he has gathered. Before that time we cannot tell if someone is good or bad, or high or low in status. We are all Adam's children, all fruits from the same tree.

Of course, there is one small difference. One fruit may be fully ripe and very tasty, another may be in the process of ripening, and another may still be as hard as rock. But we cannot hurry the unripe fruits by beating them. Each one will ripen in its own time, according to how much sun it receives and whether the wind blows on it from a southerly or northerly direction. Similarly, if we want to help the children of Adam to ripen, we can only do it by showering them with good qualities, not by beating them. We have to ripen them and make them peaceful with the kind of loving affection that regards other lives as our own.

We have been told, "Love your neighbor as you love yourself." We have not been told to beat our neighbors, to kill them, or to cut them up. That will not ripen anyone. Only if a man's heart is melting with love can he reach a state of acceptance. His heart has to be right. When we show someone love, compassion, trust, and friendship, he will melt in our embrace. Affection evokes affection. So, let us embrace our neighbors as the Prophet has taught us. Let

9. *Qiyāmah*

us share with them the things that Allah has given us. To live together in unity with all groups is the proof that we are all the children of Adam. Love your neighbor as yourself; don't take his land and kill him!

You must not accumulate wealth and destroy your good qualities. Money is a corpse. Unshakable faith, certitude, and determination is your only wealth, that is your paradise.[10] Nothing other than truth and goodness will stay with you when you die. You cannot hold on to anything else. You cannot divide up the earth and keep a share for yourself; anything taken from the earth will have to be given back to it. Nor can you divide up the waters and keep a portion as your own. You can't hold on to water. Even if you drink a thousand cupfuls, you have to eliminate it sometime. No matter how much you take, water belongs to water and earth belongs to earth.

The Prophet Muhammad gave us the laws and the words of God, but he did not seek to hold on to wealth or land or possessions in exchange. He did not want such things. All he wanted was for us to accept Allah. How did he get us to do that? By showing us good qualities. He gave us the *kalimah* and the wealth of his qualities. He told us, "This is your true wealth; this is what will help you. Take it and share it with others." The Prophet taught us to love our neighbors, to let them follow any religion they wanted to, and to be free to worship any god they chose. If our neighbors wish to come to pray with us, then we must let them come. We should never attack them. Instead, we should live with them in loving unity and be happy together.

The Prophet also taught us that one who is in Islam must never attack another who is in Islam. If there is fighting even among those who have declared the *kalimah,* think how much worse it could be among people who have not. When one who has affirmed these words attacks another who has also affirmed them, that cannot be called Islam. Anyone who has said the *kalimah* is your own flesh, for you are made from the same form.[11] You are one family, the creations of Allah, whom His light has touched. This is the absolute

---

10. *firdaws*

11. *ṣūrah*

truth, the hidden treasure that was brought to us by the Prophet.

Islam will be unified only when Muslims think like this, when they accept this oneness and act accordingly. Only then will Islam progress and this treasure grow. But when one Muslim attacks another, when one Muslim acts treacherously toward another, when a Muslim takes revenge against his neighbors or kills them, such acts hasten the destruction of the world. Should that happen and evil ways prevail, then truth, faith, the wealth of the three worlds,[12] and the grace and power[13] of the Lord of mercy of all the universes[14] will fail to benefit us. They will be wasted.

A Muslim must reflect upon the true meaning of Islam and the meaning within the divine words of the Holy Qur'an. People quote the Qur'an constantly. But is that enough? Some people can memorize the thirty sections[15] of the Qur'an in two or three years. Is that all that must be done? The Qur'an does not consist only of the words we memorize; there are countless meanings and explanations contained within those words.

We need to understand every point behind the words we read; we need to understand the meaning of every single thing we do. For example, there is an inner meaning to the *qurbān,*[16] the ritual slaughter of animals. Before the time of Muhammad, people could kill a chicken, a goat, a cow, a camel, or any other animal whenever they wanted to. They could just pick up a chicken and wring its neck. Islam put a stop to this. Instead of allowing this killing in every house at random, the people were asked to come to the mosque to have an official person slaughter the animals in the way that was permissible,[17] according to the laws.

But some people came and complained to the Prophet, saying, "My children are going without food. We waited for the official to perform the *qurbān,* but he had to go to prayers and attend to other

---

12. *mubārakāt*

13. *qudrah*

14. *raḥmat al-'ālamīn*

15. *juz'*

16. Externally, it is the ritual slaughter of animals to make them permissible to eat. Inwardly, it is to sacrifice one's life in devotion to God and to cut away the beastly qualities within the heart of man.

17. *ḥalāl*

duties, so there wasn't enough time for him to slaughter our animals.''

Muhammad then said, ''Instead of a hundred chickens, slaughter two goats. Instead of a hundred goats, slaughter ten cows. Instead of ten cows, slaughter three or four camels. Then, if you share the meat fairly, according to the size of each family, everyone will get what they need.''

The traditional stories[18] also tell of the Prophet saying to 'Alī,[19] ''Meat is one of the few foods available in our country, but if you eat the meat of any animal for forty days in a row, the qualities of that animal will come into you. 'Alī, never eat meat for forty days in a row. We should reduce our consumption of meat.'' Little by little, the Prophet gave the people these laws. Because of the strict limitations they imposed, only five to ten animals could be slaughtered a day instead of thousands. People could not simply kill as they pleased; they could take only what was needed.

Now, if the Prophet tried to reduce even the random killing of animals, should we increase the slaughter of men? How can those within a brotherhood attack and kill each other? If one person even gossips about another, and that person then gossips about the first in retaliation, fighting and death may result on all sides.

There was fighting before the Prophet brought the *kalimah,* but there is no excuse for it now. Now our neighbor is our brother, whether he recites the *kalimah* or not. We must trust him and he must trust us. We are in Islam, and that means we are in unity. The true meaning of Islam is to embrace our neighbors and love them as we love ourselves.

Each of us must think about this and look deeply into our hearts. We must pay careful attention to all of Allah's words. We must examine the inner secrets of the words of the Qur'an, the truth within every word the Prophet has spoken, and the meanings within his traditions. We must understand all that is contained within the *kalimah* and embrace each other in unity. If we can exist in that

18. *aḥādīth*

19. The fourth caliph, son-in-law of the Prophet, husband of Fatimah, and father of Ḥasan and Ḥusayn. The second convert to Islam, following Khadijah, the first wife of the Prophet.

state, we will be in Islam. That is unshakable Islam, the great treasure given by the Lord of mercy of all the universes to those of us who have received the wealth of the three worlds. Once that wealth is ours, we will see peace, harmony, and unity. That is success. May we reflect upon this.

We must always think: What is Islam? Islam is like a rose. Even if a rose has fifty petals, each one contains the same fragrance. Similarly, even if there are many millions of children in Islam, the beautiful fragrance of Allah's *kalimah* will emanate from every one of them, no matter which city or country they come from, no matter what language they speak. It will be in their words, in their thoughts, in their actions, in their faith, in their prayers, in their meditation. It will be in their *kalimah,* in their devotion,[20] in their remembrance,[21] and in their deep concentration on God.[22] That fragrance is there in the petals of every heart.[23] We must try to know that fragrance.

The blood which unites us as one is the *kalimah.* As followers of Muhammad, we must be one. That is what it means to be a true believer. If we can establish a state of unity and trust, Islam can never again descend to the state it has come to now. Today practically every Islamic country is at war with another. Wherever we look we see divisions, separations, and wars. That is not Islam.

To wage war within oneself is Islam; the real fight is an inner one. To dispel evil qualities, evil thoughts, and the differences that lead to separations is Islam. To wage war upon jealousy, envy, and vengeance is Islam. To cut out and discard the qualities of satan and to fill ourselves with the qualities of Allah is Islam. To show a heart full of love to our brothers and sisters is the wealth of Islam.

We must embrace each brother and sister with love and trust. We have to think of each one of God's qualities and fill ourselves with them, one by one, little by little. That is true love. There should

20. *'ibādah*

21. *dhikr*

22. *fikr*

23. *qalb*

not be one trace of prejudice in us. There should not be any words within us that are different from the words we speak outwardly.

The words of true Islam, the words of absolute faith, are like rays of light emerging from the sun. No matter how many clouds cover the sun, it will emerge from behind them and shine again. The clouds cannot change the sun. In the same way, the clouds of karma, sin, and satan, and the evil clouds of jealousy and revenge will come and try to conceal our light. But when faith, certitude, and determination stand firm, they will push those clouds away, and the radiant light of truth will once again shine forth from us.

To always shine with the beautiful light and form of perfect faith is Islam. And to become sweeter as we think of this is Islam. If we understand God's qualities, we will find them so sweet. If we act with God's actions, they will be sweet. When we embrace our brothers and sisters with those actions and with trust, we will realize what happiness is and know the goodness that comes from it. As we embrace each brother and sister heart to heart, helping them in whatever way they need, we will know what joy and goodness are.

As children of Adam, as members of the tribe of Abraham, as the followers of Muhammad and the disciples of Allah, we must understand this. Islam is to join together as one, knowing that those who have not affirmed the *kalimah* are our neighbors and that those who have affirmed the *kalimah* are intermingled within our own bodies.

This is the most important aspect of Islam: oneness. The tongue which says the *kalimah* makes us one. This is what must safeguard Islam. To protect our neighbors from danger is Islam. First we must see that we ourselves don't kill them, and then we must embrace them. We must act according to the laws that have been sent down, according to the words of Allah, Prophet Muhammad, and the Qur'an; the words of truth, conscience, integrity, and justice. Every thought in our hearts must follow those laws; we must not stray from them.

For a human being there are four kinds of justice: God's justice, the king's justice, man's justice, and the justice of each conscience. First we must act with God's justice. Then we must become the king inside our bodies, controlling ourselves and ruling justly over the four hundred trillion, ten thousand spiritual qualities and the millions of actions that are there within us. We must then become that king's subjects, acting with justice toward all mankind. Finally, we must develop the justice of the inner witness, the conscience, and begin to live as human beings in the state of complete justice.

We must reflect deeply on this and know what true Islam is and who we are. If we live in such a state, these qualities will spread, the *kalimah* will spread, and love, trust, and friendship will spread. Therefore, embrace every heart and make everyone your brother. Send forth from yourself the quality of embracing others and let that love touch and touch and touch their hearts, making them peaceful. That is Islam. Do not send a sword, a knife, a hatchet, or a bomb. Send the *kalimah,* send the words of the Prophet, send Allah's three thousand gracious qualities and His ninety-nine powers.[24] Send love forth from your heart to others.

If you embrace people in this way, you will realize so much happiness and sweetness, as heart after heart after heart is captured. It will turn them into exalted beings, beings of peace and tranquility. It will turn them into men of wisdom, virtuous beings with compassionate hearts. We must bring God's qualities into our actions and make them an integral part of us. We are told to feed the hungry and give charity, but giving money is not enough. Embracing others and giving them good qualities is a much greater charity. Giving wisdom is an even greater charity. And to have absolute faith and become a brother is the greatest charity of all.

Precious children, jeweled lights of my eyes, my brothers and sisters, every one of us must reflect on this and do it without fail. It must come into our understanding and live within our hearts. We must know it in our worship. It must resplend from within our inner beings and emerge from our lives as a treasure.

Islam is the greatest blessing we can receive. The treasures of Islam are the grace[25] of Allah and the wealth of all three worlds. All that we can ever understand in life is within Islam. Even our burial

---

24. *wilāyāt*

25. *raḥmah*

and the questioning in the grave and the giving of the verdict are all within Islam. It is all one.

The words I have just spoken came from my heart. They came in the name of Allah and Prophet Muhammad. They came from the innermost heart of a poor man[26] who has not studied or learned anything. Every word came from my heart. If there is any fault in what I have said, please forgive me. Every brother and sister, I most humbly beg you to forgive me in the name of Allah and the Prophet.

Amen. May the peace, the beneficence, and the blessings of God be upon you.[27]

---

26. *miskīn*

27. *al-salām 'alaykum wa-raḥmat Allāh wa-barakātuhu kulluh*

ʻIlm

Divine Knowledge

That ocean of divine knowledge contains everything: heaven, hell, this world, and the eighteen thousand universes. To know the secrets it contains, we must obtain the strength of wisdom to dive deep within it and into the depths of the qualities of God. Divine knowledge cannot be grasped by the mind. We can only understand it if we surrender to God, knowing that He is the One who can do all things.

THE OCEAN OF DIVINE KNOWLEDGE

أَعُوذُ بِٱللَّهِ مِنَ ٱلشَّيْطَانِ ٱلرَّجِيمِ بِسْمِ ٱللَّهِ ٱلرَّحْمَٰنِ ٱلرَّحِيمِ

I seek refuge in Allah from the evils of the accursed satan.
In the name of Allah, Most Merciful, Most Compassionate.

This is a small explanation of *Īmān-Islām*,[1] the way the Sufis practice it as they develop more and more clarity and wisdom.

Throughout the ages, step by step, Allah sent revelations to mankind through the prophets—through Adam, Noah, Abraham, Ishmael, Moses, David, Jesus, and all the other prophets. One prophet brought ten revelations, another brought seven, and others came with only one, two, or three.

As His final and ultimate explanation Allah sent 6,666 revelations to the Last Prophet, Muhammad, who was also the Prophet for the beginning, *Nūr Muḥammad*.[2] Those revelations are the verses of the Qur'an, and they include all the revelations sent to earlier prophets. We were provided with these explanations so that we could understand the words, conduct, and qualities of *Īmān-Islām*, and so that we could realize the value of the *kalimah*, the affirmation of faith.

Allah has given us five *kalimahs*[3] and ordained five times of prayer each day. These are essential for our peace and contentment. Earth, fire, water, air, and ether are also five in number and are necessary for the life of the body. All creations suffer when their bodies are deprived of water, when they do not have enough air to breathe, or when they feel the fire of hunger. If it is too hot the body

1. *Īmān:* absolute faith, certitude, and determination.
Islām: the state of absolute purity. See glossary.

2. The light which became completeness within Allah and then emerged.

3. See appendix.

needs something cool, if it becomes cold the body must have heat. Only after these needs are satisfied can the body feel peaceful. Similarly, only when we receive a full understanding of *Īmān-Islām* and the *kalimah* can we feel the inner peace that they offer.

God has provided all that we require to meet our inner and outer needs, at every moment, wherever we are. But in order to know exactly what will comfort us and what will quench our thirst, we have to know everything in the world of souls, in this world, and in the hereafter.[4] So that we can understand all this, Almighty God[5] has given us the Qur'an.

The Holy Qur'an is an ocean of divine knowledge.[6] It is so vast that its breadth can never be seen and its depth can never be fathomed. To try to limit it, thinking that we can ever fully comprehend its meaning, is ignorant. That ocean contains everything: heaven, hell, this world, and the eighteen thousand universes. We have been told, "Swim! Immerse yourself in that ocean of divine knowledge." To know the secrets it contains, we must obtain the strength of wisdom to dive deep within it and into the depths of the qualities of God. We must cling to the faith that the *kalimah* inspires as we repeat its words and swim with the power of the *kalimah's* radiance.

To cross this vast ocean of divine knowledge, each one of us must become a perfected human being,[7] one who lives his life with wisdom. When such a person swims, he knows. But in our present state we seem to be tied to a flimsy raft, floating on this endless ocean. With certitude we must hold fast to the oar of faith in Allah and His Messenger, knowing that Allah is the upper edge and Muhammad is the lower edge of the blade that cuts through the water and pushes us forward. Then we will be able to cross the ocean and reach the shore.

My brothers and sisters, if you can know your own life and understand it, you will find the ocean of divine knowledge within you. You will find the Qur'an within you. You are the Qur'an; you are your own book. If you can study that book and reach the state of

---

4. *al-awwal, dunyā,* and *al-ākhirah*
5. *Allāh ta'ālā*
6. *baḥr al-'ilm*
7. *insān kāmil*

fully ripened knowledge, then you will be able to speak of its sweetness and know peace and comfort in your life. To establish and understand this state is *Īmān-Islām.* To learn divine knowledge is Islam. Once we understand this, we will understand why the Prophet said, "Study divine knowledge, even if you have to go unto China."

As we mature step by step, that knowledge will reveal to us the right thing at the right time. This is how we must delve within the Qur'an. We cannot understand the Qur'an through the intellect, nor can we receive its benefits by earning titles or the esteem of the world. These things belong to satan. To try to see the value of the Qur'an with the mind is useless. The mind cannot grasp divine knowledge. That knowledge can only be understood if we surrender to God and have perfect trust in Him, knowing that He is the One who can do all things. We must study divine knowledge through the clarity of pure wisdom, with a pure soul, and through the pure qualities of inner patience, contentment, trust in God, praise of God, and the acknowledgement that God is most great and can do all things.[8]

God's beautiful qualities, duties, and actions are Islam. He is each quality, He is each duty, He is each action. He performs His duties and actions with His qualities. He is what He does. He acts, He sees, He questions, He gives, He receives. These are the meanings of His ninety-nine names.[9] These powers[10] of Allah can be found in the innermost heart[11] of each and every human being as qualities, actions, and behavior. They are the highest ideals of Islam, and they must be developed and established. Man must invite them into his heart.

When these ninety-nine powers of Allah, His three thousand divine attributes, and the qualities of His Messenger begin to resonate within the heart of a man, he will not have any enemies. When his heart is filled with the *kalimah,* when he greets his brothers with peace,[12] and when his heart sings out in supplication

---

8. *ṣabr, shukr, tawakkul 'alá Allāh, al-ḥamdu lillāh, Allāh Akbar*

9. *Asmā' al-ḥusná*

10. *wilāyāt*

11. *qalb*

12. *salām*

for God's blessings upon the prophets and upon all mankind,[13] he will see all lives as his own life. When patience, contentment, trust in God, praise of God, and the affirmation that God is great shine forth from within him, his innermost heart will resplend with unity, humility, and harmony. He will have no prejudices or differences. When the constant remembrance of and contemplation on God[14] begins to resonate in his heart, that resonance will give forth millions and millions of explanations that will bring peace to millions of hearts. Such a person will care for his neighbor as himself. He will have the ability to hold everyone in an embrace which makes them all one. He will never see anyone as an enemy, because Allah has no enemy.

Allah is each one of His names. Not one of His names has the meaning of attacking or causing pain. It is not God's work to attack others; His work is to correct what comes to Him. If something is wrong, He corrects it with His wisdom. What Allah does is Islam, and in the same way, one who is in Islam will not attack others. He will correct his own faults, so that his peaceful state will bring peace to others. He will correct his own qualities and teach God's qualities to his mind, so that those sweet qualities can soothe and comfort others. He will elevate his own state to the state of God, so that he can help others to grow.

When every heart understands this, when these qualities develop in the heart of one human being and then transfer to the hearts of other human beings, when unity and love catch every heart, every life, and every nation, then true Islam will come into being and catch fire and spread throughout the world. This is the unity that occurs when we trust and follow the words, actions, and qualities of Allah and His Messenger.

Allah has no hostility, and the *kalimah* brought by His Prophet expresses no hostility. Once we say that *kalimah* and accept the truth of God with absolute faith, we will see everyone and everything as Islam. Drawing a sword, attacking others, or trying to force them into our beliefs is not Islam. True Islam means controlling

---

13. *ṣalawāt*

14. *dhikr* and *fikr*

ourselves, controlling the anger, jealousy, and vengeance that come from our own minds, and attacking all the thoughts within us that hurt others. That is the war we all must wage.

God has no need to wage wars. He is capable of creating or destroying universes within the blink of an eye. If He were to close His eye, nothing would exist; when it opened again, creation would come back to life. Similarly, in the blink of an eye, the darkness within the heart can be dispelled and the light of God's qualities can come back to life.

Is-lām. Lām[15] is light, the light of the pure soul and pure wisdom. The word Islam describes a place where there is no darkness at all, a place where there are no differences, no disputes over races or religions, a place where there is only light. As we open our eyes and our hearts to that light, to inner patience, and to the wisdom of divine knowledge, all our evil tendencies will be burned away, and all of God's beauty will come into being within us.

Of course, if we do not recognize the difference between good and evil, we might burn everything indiscriminately. But if we apply our understanding we will burn away only the bad. Then light will come into being, and we will see the power of God's grace and understand what Islam truly is. One who understands this will gain the wealth of the three worlds.[16] For such a man, this world is heaven, the hereafter is heaven, and even the time of creation, of birth, is heaven. *Īmān-Islām* is the name given to this state when it is established with awareness. But as long as we do not understand this properly and continue to say, "I am great, I am greater than you," we have not reached that level of understanding. Only when we have rid ourselves of all our blemishes will we be able to see God.

My brothers and sisters, even though we have not yet seen God, there is no place where He does not exist. He is within every life. He is in the trees, the flowers, the fruits, and in the plants and shrubs

15. The Arabic letter (ل) which correlates to the English consonant 'l'. In the transformed man of wisdom, *lām* represents the resplendence, or *Nūr,* of Allah.

16. *mubārakāt*

and vines. There would be no flowers or fruits on a tree if His power did not exist within it. When we squeeze a fruit its sweet juice can quench our thirst and satisfy our hunger, because it has His power within it.

The same intensity of sweetness exists within the ideals of Islam. If we accept the qualities of Allah and Prophet Muhammad, as we affirm our faith with the *kalimah* and embrace our brothers in peace and unity, and as we sing a prayer for God's blessings upon the prophets and all mankind, we will experience that sweetness. The trust inspired by that love will melt our hearts and touch the hearts of everyone around us. We will be like honeybees collecting the nectar from a million flowers and storing it within our hearts. Islam is the honey that unites, the honey that we can taste and enjoy and share with everyone else. Once we are filled with that honey, we will embrace all lives as our own, in unity. Our racial and religious prejudices will leave us. Doubt, jealousy, and the spilling of blood will cease. When that sweetness of *Īmān-Islām* comes into us we will see Islam in everyone.

All of creation is within Islam. God created everything and everyone as Islam, as light. Who is not in Islam? Since the time of Adam everything has been in Islam. Adam, Noah, Abraham, Ishmael, Moses, David, Jesus, and Muhammad are all within Islam. Idris, Isaac, Job, Jacob, Salih, and the many other prophets are also within Islam. Everyone created is embraced within Islam. God never called anyone anything else. It is we who call ourselves by different races and different tribes. It is our arrogance that causes destruction. It destroys us and it destroys others. As long as we do not reach that state of divine knowledge, wisdom, and clarity, only trouble will arise. We will end up fighting each other and bringing great harm to each other.

Wisdom means not hurting anyone. We should embrace one another with patience. And if our difficulties increase, we must be contented and continue to embrace each other. If things become even more difficult, the sweetness of our embrace must deepen and we must have trust in God, surrendering to Him saying, "All praise is to You! I have done as much as I can, it is Your responsibility now. I praise You!" And if the situation becomes impossible, we must say, "*Allāh Akbar,* You are the greatest. I die within You. Accept me."

Patience, contentment, trust in God, praising God's greatness and His power—those qualities are the honey, the taste of the fruit of Islam. Through them you can reach the highest level of *Īmān-Islām* and find contentment in life. Then we will be able to comfort others and help them find the treasure of peace that the world is now lacking.

My love you. May God help us. May the peace and blessings of God be with you.[17] Amen.

17. *al-salām 'alaykum*

أُمُّ القُرآن

Umm al-Qur'ān

The mother of man's wisdom

Allah and the state of a true human being exists right here as a great silent mystery within our innermost hearts, within the Umm al-Qur'ān. *What does* umm *mean? Mother. It is the mother of man's wisdom, of justice and faith, the mother who raises the true believer.*

THE INNER QUR'AN

اَعُوذُ بِاللّٰهِ مِنَ الشَّيْطَانِ الرَّجِيمِ بِسْمِ اللّٰهِ الرَّحْمٰنِ الرَّحِيمِ

I seek refuge in Allah from the evils of the accursed satan.
In the name of Allah, Most Merciful, Most Compassionate.

May all the peace, the beneficence, and the blessings of God be upon you.[1]

Brothers and sisters in Islam, no matter what changes occur throughout the ages, the Qur'an is one thing that never changes. It is immutable. It offers an explanation appropriate for every period of time and for every level of understanding. All the meanings it contains could not be written down even if all the oceans of the world were made into ink and all the trees were made into pens.

To comprehend the Qur'an, first we must establish our absolute faith, certitude, and determination;[2] then we must acquire wisdom; and finally we must delve deep inside and study it from within. If we look into the depths of the Qur'an, we will find the complete never-ending wealth and grace of Almighty God.[3] We will find the light of Allah, the resplendence of Allah. We will not find racial or religious prejudices, battles, or fighting of any kind. We will find only the benevolence of all the universes.

The Qur'an appeared as the beginning, the emergence of creation (*Awwal Muḥammad*), as the eternal life, the emergence of the soul (*Hayāh Muḥammad*), as the food, the nourishment for all creations (*An'um Muḥammad*), as the innermost heart (*Aḥmad*), as the beauty of the face which is a reflection of the beauty of the heart (*Muḥammad*), and as the plenitude, the light which became completeness within Allah and then emerged (*Nūr Muḥammad*).

1. *al-salām 'alaykum wa-raḥmat Allāh wa-barakātuhu kulluh*
2. *īmān*
3. The *raḥmah* of *Allāh ta'ālá*.

The Qur'an is a treasure which continually speaks to our faith. Its verses were sent to Muhammad one by one, according to the needs of the people, the difficulties they were undergoing, and the questions they asked. These verses and chapters were sent to bring clarity to man, from the time he appears as a fetus, as the *mīm,*[4] to the moment he reaches the shore of the hereafter. They cleanse man stage by stage. Whatever state he is in at one time of prayer,[5] the Qur'an explains the state he should achieve by the next prayer time. In this way, the Qur'an lifts man up, causing his wisdom, his beauty, and his divine knowledge[6] to grow little by little.

The Prophet said, "Even though I depart from the world, I leave you the Qur'an. That is your evidence. Please keep it close to you. The Qur'an will be a teacher and a learned one to the innermost heart." That is why its verses were sent to mankind. Step by step the Qur'an elevates man; chapter by chapter, it cuts away all the things within him that need to be discarded. That is the purpose of the Qur'an—to eliminate the four hundred trillion, ten thousand degenerate qualities and actions which oppose the truth of God, and to show man how to develop, how to beautify and improve himself. The Qur'an has the capacity to cut away this birth, to cast out arrogance, karma, illusion, and the sexual energies of the three sons of illusion.[7] It can dispel man's love for earth, sensual pleasures, and gold. It can drive away lust, anger, miserliness, attachment, bigotry, envy, theft, murder, falsehood, and the effects of intoxicants.

To rid himself of these evil qualities, a true human being must sacrifice and purify his heart for Allah. He must perform the ritual sacrifice called *qurbān*[8] for the sake of truth and justice, for the sake

4. *mīm,* the Arabic letter (م) which correlates to the English consonant 'm' Its shape is similar to the sperm cell. See glossary.

5. *waqt*

6. *ilm*

7. *tārahan:* the pathway for the sexual act, the birth canal or vagina.
singhan: the arrogance present at the moment of ejaculation.
sūran: the illusory images of the mind enjoyed during the sexual act.

8. Externally, it is the ritual slaughter of animals to make them permissible to eat. Inwardly, it is to sacrifice one's life in devotion to God and to cut away the beastly qualities within the heart of man.

of righteous action, duty, equality, peacefulness, unity, and for the love of the one human family. If he does this, he will acquire the qualities, actions, and beauty of Allah. This is the state which the Qur'an depicts, the path of perfect purity.[9] This is Allah's kingdom, and He is the only One who protects it, conducts its affairs, and rules over it with total justice. Anyone who acts according to that justice and understands Allah in completeness becomes His slave.[10] Such a man owns nothing of his own, and so Allah protects him and looks after all his needs.

If a man progresses to this state of purity, if he succeeds in cutting away all these evil qualities, then he becomes a true believer,[11] living for nothing other than Allah, and having nothing other than Allah in his thoughts or intentions. He does not concern himself with seeing or hearing others, because no one else exists for him. He sees nothing other than Allah. He speaks to no one other than Allah. He has closed himself off to the sight and sound of everything but Allah. That is why he is called an *ummī,* an unlettered one. And because he has no words of his own, Allah's words and sounds come through him. He becomes the *ḥadīth*[12] which explains the inner and outer aspects of Allah's revelations. In that state, his body or form is the holy book and his innermost heart is the *Umm al-Qur'ān.* What does *Umm* mean? It means mother. The mother who raises the true believer is the *Umm al-Qur'ān,* the mother of justice and faith, the mother of man's wisdom. The *Umm al-Qur'ān* is the essence of the Qur'an, the eye of the Qur'an.

If man will only open that eye, he will know Allah, and knowing Allah, he will hear only His sounds and His words. This was the state of the Prophet, *Muḥammad al-Ummī.* He was unlearned, and therefore, the words that he received could only have come through God's revelation.[13] Allah explained to Muhammad the meaning of

---

9. *Dīn al-Islām*

10. *'abd*

11. *mu'min*

12. The traditions of Prophet Muhammad, often the words and commands of God. In this context, man becomes Allah's words and sounds.

13. *waḥy*

Īmān-Islām, prayer, worship,[14] and everything He had revealed to the earlier prophets. Through Muhammad, His Final Prophet, Allah clarified everything for mankind.

Of all the prophets, only Moses and Muhammad attained the state where they met and spoke directly to God—Moses on Mount Sinai, when God revealed Himself as a resplendent light, and Muhammad once face to face during his mystical journey to heaven,[15] and also in the many direct revelations he received.[16]

Moses and Muhammad also shared another distinction. They were the only two prophets whose names began with the letter *mīm.* The *mīm* was what Allah created first, and from it He made all of His creations. The letter *mīm* covers the universes of the primal beginning, this world, and the hereafter.[17] It penetrates the essence and the manifestation,[18] as well as good and evil. All creations begin with *mīm,* and as long as they continue to appear, that *mīm,* the pearl of creation, will exist. It is endless.

Through that *mīm* Allah gave Moses the Ten Commandments and the explanations of the Torah, showing him what was permissible and forbidden[19] according to God's law, and what was good and evil.[20] With the grace of that *mīm,* Moses was able to perform miracles and to deliver his people from Pharoah. And it was to the *mīm* in Muhammad that Allah revealed the 6,666 verses of the Qur'an.

The Sufis say that it is impossible to give a complete explanation of the *mīm;* it can only be grasped by those who search deeply with perfect faith and an open heart. How then is it possible to explain who Muhammad truly is? How can we say when Muhammad was created or when he appeared? Only if we understand the real Qur'an completely can we understand Muhammad. Until a man reaches that state, he will continue to say that Muhammad is the son of Āminah and 'Abdullah. The Sufis call Muhammad the light of the innermost heart. In Tamil *muham* means face and *aham* means

---

14. *salāh* and *'ibādah*
15. *mi'rāj*
16. *ḥadīth qudsī*
17. *al-awwal, dunyā,* and *al-ākhirah*
18. *dhāt* and *ṣifāt*
19. *ḥalāl* and *ḥarām*
20. *khayr* and *sharr*

heart. When the *Aḥmad*, the state of the heart, becomes Muhammad, then the light of the innermost heart is revealed in the beauty of the face.

The Sufis also say that only when man comes to a realization of himself and dives deep within the inner Qur'an, drinking from its essence, will the truth of Muhammad be revealed to him in his meditation. Only when he reaches the state where he speaks to Allah alone, can he be said to truly exist in Islam. When he attains that state of communion with Allah, he will understand that the Qur'an and the holy books are his own body, the inner mystical form of a true human being. Such a man will understand the inner meaning of *al-ḥamdu lillāh,*[21] which is the praise of the inner form of man. Understanding the history of the One who is all praise, he will glorify Him alone. Only then can he see this history as one continuous study, an endless ocean of divine knowledge. Otherwise, each book he reads will explain a few points and then refer him to another book which will then refer him to yet another book. As long as he continues reading only those outer books, he will never reach his freedom.

My brothers, we must consider how the Qur'an came from Allah, and we must delve deep within it. In order to understand its true meaning, we must be in the same state as that original Qur'an was when it emerged from Allah. It came as a resplendence, a radiance, a resonance, and a grace. Then it came as a light to Gabriel. And when it came to Muhammad, the Messenger, it came as the grace and attributes of Allah. Next Muhammad brought it to us as a revelation. Then the sound of these revelations was transformed into letters and formed into words. What was revealed in those words ultimately became public knowledge and part of history. The interpretations of this knowledge later gave rise to religious differences, divisions, and bigotry, which in turn gave rise to prejudice, fighting, and wars. This is the state the world has come to.

We, however, must delve into the depths of the Qur'an; we must experience each step of the way as it originally came from Allah. As

21. All praise is to God!

we look deeper and deeper, we will see the Messenger of God, and once we see him, we will know how Gabriel came to him and how he received that grace. We will see the light, and if we look through that light we will experience the resonance of Allah within the Qur'an. As we understand that resonance, we will understand our life and our death; we will understand the Day of Judgment, the Day of Questioning, and the ninety-nine attributes[22] of Allah.

Once we have this understanding, we will see that all men are our brothers, just as the Qur'an teaches us. To truly see all people as our brothers is Islam. If we see anyone who is in need, we must offer him the water of the mercy of all the universes, the water of absolute faith, and the affirmation of that faith, the ***kalimah***. That water must be given to everyone who is hungry or thirsty. We must embrace them lovingly, quench their thirst, and wash away their dirt. We must offer them love, compassion, patience, and tolerance, just as the Prophet did. This is what will satisfy their needs and dispel the darkness in their hearts.

My brothers and sisters in Islam, if we offer peace, then justice will flourish. Love will cut away all enmity. Compassion will cause God's grace to grow in this world, and then the food of faith and the mercy of all the universes can be offered. When that food is given, hunger, disease, old age, and death will be eliminated, and everyone will have peace.

Allah and the state of a true human being are right here within us. It is a great secret, hidden within our hearts, within the *Umm al-Qur'ān*. Only if we can study this divine knowledge can we attain our freedom. All who have faith must reflect upon this, understand it, and teach it to those who have less wisdom, to those who have no clarity of heart, to those whose minds oppose us, and to those who have no peace of mind. We must teach them these qualities, give them this food, this beauty, and this nourishment of grace and absolute faith. Every human being in the community of Islam, everyone who has faith, all those who are learned and wise, all the leaders of prayer and the teachers, all those who know the Qur'an—all must understand this. This is what I ask of you.

Amen. Allah is sufficient unto us all.

---

22. *wilāyāt*

يَا سَمِيعُ

Yā Samī‘

O All-Hearing One

To all who say they believe in God, please realize with your faith that God hears every word you say. God hears your every thought. Realizing this, speak only what is truth and act only with God's qualities of love, compassion, justice, patience, and the realization that each life is as important as your own.

THE TRUE MEANING OF ISLAM

أَعُوذُ بِاللّٰهِ مِنَ الشَّيْطَانِ الرَّجِيمِ بِسْمِ اللّٰهِ الرَّحْمٰنِ الرَّحِيمِ

I seek refuge in Allah from the evils of the accursed satan.
In the name of Allah, Most Merciful, Most Compassionate.

In the name of God, the Most Merciful and Most Compassionate.

May all praise be for God alone. May we give the entire responsibility for our lives to that one God who is limitless grace and incomparable love. May the peace of God and all His blessings fill the lives of all who may read this message.

To all who say they believe in God, please realize with your faith that God hears every word you say. God hears your every thought. Realizing this, speak only what is truth and act only with God's qualities of love, compassion, justice, patience, and the realization that each life is as important as your own. This is the true message within the Qur'an. The Qur'an does not cause divisions among God's children. It exists to bring about brotherhood and unity. The Qur'an soothes those who weep in sorrow and gives comfort to those who suffer. To those who may be poor, it explains the bounteous wealth of God. It inspires faith in those who may not have believed in God and helps them reach a state of reverence for God.

Do not wave the words of the Qur'an as though they were a banner you were going to carry into battle. Do not say, "The Qur'an says this and the Qur'an says that," without truly understanding the inner wisdom of God's qualities within your own life. If one has faith, certitude, and determination,[1] he will see the seed of that purity that is Islam within everything. He will see the power of Allah in every creation.

Therefore, he will not discriminate against another creation or

1. *īmān*

discard him. Anyone who has the purity of Islam and that true faith, certitude, and determination within his heart cannot hurt the heart of another in any manner. Instead, he will have the patience of God in dealing with others; he will use his gratitude to God as the strength with which to comfort others; his praise for God will be the wealth he will share with others; and his total trust in God will be his own wealth, contentment, and security. He will consider anything that does not exist as the quality of God (known in Islam as Allah's ninety-nine names or powers) as forbidden, or evil. Only that which exists within those divine qualities is permissible, or good.

These attributes of the grace of God are the law of the Qur'an. These divine attributes are the law within the heart of one who has true faith, certitude, and determination and is truly Islam. The capture of other lives and attacks against other countries are not the law. Muhammad, the Messenger of God,[2] did not keep anything other than God. From the time of his appearance until the time he departed, the only wealth the Messenger of God displayed and the only power he showed was the wealth and the power of God's qualities of compassion and grace.

Children of any religion who have true faith must realize that God is the only One who knows all of everything. Therefore, only God can judge whether a person has faith, certitude, and determination or not and whether a person lives with that purity that can be called Islam or not. No one else can give that judgment. Do not wave your religion like a banner and go out to capture others. Only one kind of war is permissible in the eyes of God: the war you wage within yourself to defeat the demonic forces of lust, anger, jealousy, desire for revenge, and other evil feelings and attributes that may exist within your heart. God has sent each of the prophets as witnesses to the grace of God and as supports to help us in this inner war. This is the reason for the Qur'an. It is to help the true Muslim fight this inner battle and win victory over his own base desires[3] that God sent the Messenger with the Qur'an. We must use the wisdom contained within the Qur'an to spank our own naughty minds and

---

2. *Rasūl Allāh*

3. *nafs*

defeat our own compulsive desires. If we do that, what is called Islam will taste like honey. What we do now by battling in the world and calling it Islam tastes bitter and covers the light of the Qur'an in darkness.

The light of Islam should reveal the essence of God in every life. If we see that essence, then we will live in unity; we will eat from the same plate; we will live as one family whether some are in a church, some are in a mosque, or some are in their homes. The beggar and the king will be able to pray together. We will discover our own faults, discard our own anger, and embrace one another with love. That is what the Qur'an says. That is why we cannot tell lies, indulge in treachery, or threaten to kill other lives and claim that it is being done in the name of Islam. Islam teaches that we must recognize and praise the essence of God as it exists in each and every life.

Consider this explanation of the truth that is in the Qur'an: If you take a tiny atom and split it into ten million particles and take one of these particles and examine it with that true wisdom found within Islam, you will see within that tiny particle ninety-nine particles revolving around one another without touching. (The ninety-nine are those qualities of God's grace that are known as the names, or powers, of God.) If you take one of those ninety-nine particles and split it into five million particles and examine one of those pieces with that wisdom, again you will see ninety-nine—ninety-nine revolving around one another without touching. And if you take any one of those particles and split it into one million pieces and examine one piece, again you will see the ninety-nine particles revolving around one another. If you take one of those and split it into five hundred thousand pieces and take one of those particles and split it into two hundred and fifty thousand pieces and take one of those and split it into one hundred thousand pieces and then one of those into ten thousand pieces and one of those into another thousand pieces and if you take one of those infinitesimal particles and look within it with that wisdom, you will see ninety-nine: His ninety-nine divine powers.[4] Every particle of every atom contains the power of Allah, the divine power of God. We who are Islam must

4. *wilāyāt*

realize this. If we reflect on this, anyone who calls himself Islam will never harm anyone. He will not wreak revenge. He will not be treacherous toward anyone. Islam must realize this. Everyone who has faith in God must realize this.

All children of God, leave behind all lustful desires and come to the plenitude of firm faith in God. Give up anger and come to the house of patience. Give up the tendency toward vengeance and treachery and come into the house of contentment with God's wealth of grace. Give up the hell caused by your attachment to the world and come into the love of God that is His grace. Only when you incorporate His ninety-nine compassionate powers as the basis for your actions and as the law for your life can you discover even one atom—one tiny particle—of God's mercy and compassion.

In the name of God, the Most Merciful and Most Compassionate. May all praise and praising be to God alone, and may we have His peace in our hearts. Amen.

رَبُّ الْعَالَمِينَ

Rabb al-'ālamīn

Lord of all the universes

Our entire life and everything that happens to us is conducted by Allah, not by us. He is the One who carries out everything. He is responsible for the cause and the effect.

EPILOGUE

اَعُوذُبِاللّهِ مِنَ الشَّيْطَانِ الرَّجِيمِ بِسْمِ اللّهِ الرَّحْمٰنِ الرَّحِيمِ

I seek refuge in Allah from the evils of the accursed satan.
In the name of Allah, Most Merciful, Most Compassionate.

May all the peace, the beneficence, and the blessings of God be upon you.[1]

My brothers and sisters, let us consider once more the true meaning of Islam.

Islam is Allah. It is the kingdom of His qualities, His actions, His compassion, His peacefulness, and His unity. Allah, not man, is the only One who can rule that kingdom. With His love and compassion He is the One who protects all lives, who feeds and looks after all creations according to their needs and their hunger. Allah alone rules over all that is within His realm—the earth and all the countries of the world, the trees, plants, the houses, and the heart of man. Our entire life and everything that happens to us is conducted by Allah, not by us. He is the One who carries out everything, He is responsible for the cause and the effect.

Islam is the acceptance of Allah as the Ruler over everything in all the universes.[2] He is the Master of our good thoughts, our good qualities, and our good actions. He is the Guide for our conscience, the One who teaches us justice and truth, compassion and unity. He is the Leader of wisdom and divine knowledge.[3] And it is through His peace that all hearts can obtain peace and tranquility.

His is the kingdom of truth. That kingdom cannot be ruled by

---

1. *al-salām 'alaykum wa-raḥmat*
   Allāh wa-barakātuhu kulluh

2. *Rabb al-'ālamīn*

3. *'ilm*

what the world today calls Islam. True Islam does not mean trying to dominate the world, shouting, "I am in command!" In this world and the next, in birth and in death, the One alone who rules Islam is Allah. No man has the power to govern that kingdom.

To understand this with absolute clarity is to become His slave[4] and be filled with divine wisdom and perfect faith. That is prayer. To accept Allah and His pure kingdom is true Islam, the way of absolute faith, certitude, and determination,[5] the way of the *kalimah*.[6] This is the birthright of all the children of Adam. To accept Allah's words and His commands is wisdom, and to accept what He has given us is our plenitude.

God is Most Great![7] All praise belongs only to Him.[8] He is the One who gives us the wealth of our lives. He gives us everything. The kingdom of Islam is His most benevolent, pure gift. Should any man proclaim himself ruler of that pure kingdom, he will only bring about his own destruction. Allah is the sole ruler, there is no one else who can do His work. We, the children of Adam, who pray to God with faith and certitude, must know this with absolute clarity.

All praise be to God! God is the Great One! This is the true meaning of Islam.

May the peace of God be upon us. May God help us all. Amen.

---

4. *'abd*

5. *īmān*

6. The affirmation of faith.

7. *Allāh Akbar*

8. *al-ḥamdu lillāh*

Appendix

al-Kalimāt al-Khams
THE FIVE KALIMAHS

al-Kalimah al-Ūlá
THE FIRST KALIMAH

Lā ilāh illā Allāh; Muḥammad Rasūl Allāh.
None is god except Allah; Muhammad is the Messenger of Allah.

al-Kalimah al-Thāniyah
(al-shahādah)
THE SECOND KALIMAH
(The Testimony of Faith)

Ashhadu an lā ilāh illā Allāh waḥdahu lā sharīk lahu,
wa-ashhadu anna Muḥammad ʻabduhu wa-rasūluh.
I testify that none is god except Allah, He is One without associates to Him; and I testify that Muhammad is His servant and His Messenger.

al-Kalimah al-Thālithah
THE THIRD KALIMAH

Subḥān Allāh wa-al-ḥamd lillāh wa-lā ilāh illā Allāh wa-Allāh akbar wa-lā ḥawla wa-lā qūwah illā billāh al-ʻAlī, al-ʻAẓīm.
Glory is Allah's, and all praise is Allah's, and none is god except Allah, and Allah is most great! And there is no majesty or power except in Allah, and He is exalted, supremely magnificent!

al-Kalimah al-Rābi'ah
THE FOURTH KALIMAH

Lā ilāh illā Allāh waḥdahu lā sharīk lahu; lahu al-mulk wa-lahu al-ḥamd; yuḥyī wa-yumītu; bi yadihi al-khayr wa-huwa 'alá kull shay' qadīr.

None is god except Allah, He is One without associates to Him. His is the dominion and His is the praise; He bestows life and death, in His hand are the blessings, and He is omnipotent over all things.

al-Kalimah al-Khāmisah
THE FIFTH KALIMAH

Allāhumma, innī a'udhu bi-ka min an ushrika bi-ka shay' wa-ana a'lamu wa-astaghfiruka li-mā lā a'lamu innaka Anta 'Alim al-ghaib wa-al-shahādah. Tubtu 'anhu wa-tabarra'tu 'an kull dīn siwá Dīn al-Islām, wa-aslamtu laka wa-aqūlu: lā ilāh illā Allāh, Muḥammad Rasūl Allāh.

Dearest Allah! I seek protection in Thee against ascribing any partner to Thee knowingly, and I beg Thy forgiveness for that which I might do unknowingly—indeed, Thou art the Knower of both what is seen and what is hidden. I have turned from such faults and I absolve myself from every sort of creed except pure belief in and surrender to Thee, and I commit myself wholly to Thee saying, None is god but Allah! Muhammad is the Messenger of Allah!

Glossary

(A) Indicates an Arabic word

(T) Indicates a Tamil word

'abd (A) A slave.

aḥādīth (A) (sing. *ḥadīth*) Traditions of the Prophet Muhammad; traditional stories.

aham (T) The heart. Muhammad can be defined as the beauty of the heart [*aham*] reflected in the face [*muham*].

aḥmad (A) The state of the heart, the *qalb,* or *aham*. *Aḥmad* is the heart of Muhammad. The beauty of the heart [*aham*] is the beauty of the countenance [*muham,* Tamil] of Muhammad. That is the beauty of Allah's qualities. This is a name that comes from within the ocean of divine knowledge [*baḥr al-'ilm*]. Allah is the One who is worthy of the praise of the *qalb,* the heart. Lit.: most praiseworthy.

al-ākhirah (A) The hereafter; the next world; the kingdom of God.

'ālam (A) (pl. *'ālamūn* or *'ālamīn*) The universe; the cosmos; the metaphysical world.

'ālam al-arwāḥ (A) The world of pure souls, where all souls are performing *tasbīḥ,* or prayers of praise to God.

al-ḥamdu lillāh (A) "All praise is to You." Allah is the glory and greatness that deserves all praise. "You are the One responsible for the appearance of all creations. Whatever appears, whatever disappears, whatever receives benefit or loss—all is Yours. I have surrendered everything into Your hands. I remain with hands outstretched, spread out, empty, and helpless. Whatever is happening and whatever is going to happen is all Yours." Lit.: All praise belongs to Allah!

alif (A) The first letter of the Arabic alphabet (ا). To the transformed man of wisdom, the *alif* represents Allah, the One. See also: *lām, mīm*.

'ālim (A) (pl. *'ulamā'*) Teacher; learned one; one of wisdom. One who swims in Allah's *dhāt* [essence of grace] and has learned the ocean of divine knowledge [*baḥr al-'ilm*].

Allāh Akbar (A) God is Great!

Allāh ta'ālá (A) God Almighty; God is the Highest. *Allāh:* (A) the beautiful undiminishing One. *Ta'ālá:* (A) the One who exists in all lives in a state of humility and exaltedness.

Amīr al-Mu'minīn (A) Commander of the faithful.

anbiyā' (A) (sing. *nabī*) Prophets.

An'um Muḥammad (A) The food; the *rizq;* the nourishment of all creations; Muḥammad of the kindnesses or blessings.

'arsh (A) The throne of God; the plenitude from which God rules. The station located on the crown of the head which is the throne that can bear the weight of Allah. Allah is so heavy that we cannot carry the load with our hands or legs. The *'arsh* is the only part of man that can support Allah.

'arsh al-mu'min (A) The throne of the true believer; the throne of one who has steadfast *īmān* [absolute faith, certitude, and determination]; the throne of an *insān,* a true man who has that perfect certitude of *īmān.* Allah resides within the heart which praises Him, the tongue which speaks only virtuous thoughts, the tongue which speaks the truth and praises the truth.

aṣḥāb (A) Companions of Prophet Muhammad.

Asmā' al-ḥusnā (A) The ninety-nine beautiful names of Allah. The plenitude of the ninety-nine duties of God; the *ṣifāt* of His *dhāt,* the manifestations of His essence. The states of His qualities are His manifestations which emerge from Him. He performs His duty when these manifestations of His essence are brought into action. Then they become His *wilāyāt,* the actions which stem from the manifestations of His essence.

The *Asmā' al-ḥusnā* are the ninety-nine beautiful names of His duties. They were revealed to Prophet Muhammad in the Qur'an, and he explained them to his followers. This is a vast *baḥr al-dawlah,* a very deep ocean of His grace and His limitless, infinite, and undiminishing wealth.

If we go on cutting one of these ninety-nine *wilāyāt* over and over again, taking one piece at a time, we will see ninety-nine particles revolving one around the other without touching. This applies to each one of the ninety-nine *wilāyāt.* This is the *Asmā' al-ḥusnā.* As we go on cutting, we lose ourselves in that. We die within that.

How can we ever hope to reach an end of the ninety-nine? If we receive only one drop of that, it will be more than sufficient for us. The person who has touched the smallest, tiniest drop becomes a good one. These are merely His powers. If you go on cutting just one of His powers, it is so powerful that it will draw you in. That power will swallow you up, and you become the power [*wilāyah*]. Then you come to the stage at which you can lose yourself within Allah; you can disappear within Allah.

'aṣr (A) The third of the five-times prayers; also means era, time, and afternoon.

astaghfiru Allāh al-'Aẓīm (A) I seek forgiveness from Allah the Supreme.

a'ūdhu billāhi min al-Shayṭān al-Rajīm (A) I seek refuge in God from the evils of the accursed Satan.

awliyā' (A)(sing. *walī*) The favorites of God. Those who are near to God, referring to holy men of Islam.

al-awwal (A) The creation of all forms; the stage at which the soul became surrounded by form and each creation took shape; the stage at which the souls of the six kinds of lives (earth-life, fire-life, water-life, air-life, ether-life, and light-life) were placed in their respective forms. Allah created these forms and then placed that 'trust property' which is life within those forms.

Awwal Muḥammad (A) The first Muhammad; the beginning; the emergence of creation; the time Muhammad emerged, resonated, and pulsated within Allah.

baḥr al-'ilm (A) The ocean of divine knowledge.

barakat (A) The wealth of Allah's grace.

al-Bayt al-Muqaddas: A name given to the temple at Jerusalem, on which site the Dome of the Rock stands today. Lit.: the Holy House.

Bismillāh al-Raḥmān al-Raḥīm (A) In the name of God, Most Merciful, Most Compassionate. *Bismillāh:* Allah is the first and the last, the One with the beginning and without beginning. He is the One who is the cause for creation and for the absence of creation, the cause for the beginning and for the beginningless.

al-Raḥmān: He is the King, the Nourisher, the One who gives food. He is the Compassionate One. He is the One who protects the creations. He is the Beneficent One.

al-Raḥīm: He is the One who redeems, the One who protects from evil, who preserves and who confers eternal bliss; the Savior. On the Day of Judgment and on the Day of Inquiry and on all days from the day of the beginning, He protects and brings His creations back unto Himself.

Dajjāl (A) Antichrist. Lit.: lying, false.

dawlah (A) This has two meanings. One is the wealth of the world, or *dunyā.* The other is the wealth of the grace of Allah. The wealth of Allah is the wealth of the divine knowledge known as *'ilm* and the wealth of perfect *īmān,* or absolute faith, certitude, and determination.

dhāt (A) The essence of God; His treasury; His wealth of purity; His grace.

dhikr (A) The remembrance of God. It is a common name given to certain words in praise of God. Of the many *dhikrs,* the most exalted *dhikr* is to say, "*Lā ilāh illā Allāh*—There is nothing other than You. Only You are Allah." All the others relate to His *wilāyāt,* or His actions, but this *dhikr* points to Him and to Him alone. See also: *kalimah; Lā ilāh illā Allāh.*

dīn (A) The light of perfect purity; the resplendence of perfectly pure *īmān,* absolute faith, certitude, and determination. Lit.: religion, faith, or belief.

Dīn al-Islām (A) The faith of surrender to the will of Allah.

dunyā (A) The earth-world in which we live; the world of physical existence; the darkness which separated from Allah at the time when the light of the *Nūr Muḥammad* manifested from within Allah.

fikr (A) Contemplation; meditation; concentration on God.

firdaws (A) The eighth heaven. If we can cut away the seven base desires known as the *nafs ammārah,* what remains will be Allah's qualities, actions, and conduct, His gracious attributes, and His duties. If man can make these his own and store them within his heart, then that is *firdaws*. That is Allah's house, the limitless heaven. That will be the eighth heaven, Allah's house of infinite magnitude and perfect purity.

furūḍ (A) (sing. *farḍ*) The five *furūḍ* refer to the five pillars of Islam: *Īmān,* or absolute faith, prayer, charity, fasting, and *ḥajj,* or holy pilgrimage.

gnānam (T) Divine luminous wisdom; grace-awakened wisdom. If man can throw away all the worldly treasures and take within him only the treasure called Allah and His qualities and actions, His conduct and behavior, if he makes Allah the only treasure and completeness for him—that is the state of *gnānam.*

ḥadīth (A) (pl. *aḥādīth*) A tradition of the Prophet Muhammad; traditional story.

ḥadīth qudsī (A) A divine transmission directly revealed to Prophet Muhammad without Gabriel as an intermediary.

ḥajj (A) A pilgrimage; the fifth *farḍ,* or obligatory duty, in Islam.

"Do this duty wearing the *kafan,* the shroud, like one who has died to the world. Give a share of your wealth to those who are poor. If you have a wife and children, divide your wealth among them. Even the inner desires must be surrendered—all of the self must die for the *ḥajj.*"

ḥalāl (A) That which is permissible or lawful according to the commands of God and which conforms to the word of God. This relates to both food and to divine knowledge, or *'ilm.*

ḥarām (A) That which is forbidden by truth and forbidden by the warnings or commands of God. For those who are on the straight path, *ḥarām* means all the evil things, the actions, the food, and the dangers that can obstruct the path.

ḥayāh (A) The plenitude of man's eternal life; the splendor of the completeness of life; the *rūḥ,* or the soul, of the splendor of man's life.

Ḥayāh Muḥammad (A) Life of Muhammad.

ḥayf (A) A wrong; a harm; damage; injustice; having faults.

ḥikmah (A) Divine wisdom.

'ibādah (A) Worship and service to the One God.

iḥsān (A) To do right and to act beautifully, because one knows that Allah is always watching man's actions and thoughts.

'ilm (A) Allah's divine knowledge.

imām (A) Leader of prayer.

Imām Abū Ḥanīfah, Imām Mālik, Imām Ibn Ḥanbal, Imām al-Shāfi'ī (A) The four *imāms:*

Imām Abū Ḥanīfah: Born in al-Kufah A.H. 80 and died in Baghdad A.H. 150.
Imām Mālik: Born and died in Medina A.H. 94-A.H. 179.
Imām Ibn Ḥanbal: Born and died in Baghdad A.H. 164-A.H. 241.
Imām al-Shāfi'ī: Born in Askalon, Pakistan A.H. 150 and died in Cairo A.H. 204.

These four men systematically developed the rules of conduct and law [*fiqh*] from the injunctions of the Qur'an and the *aḥādīth.* Four different schools of thought were established after them and each has a slightly different interpretation of the practices of Islam.

Imām al-Ghazzāli revealed in *Ihyā' 'Ulūm al-Dīn* that all four men not only devoted themselves to the knowledge of jurisprudence [*fiqh*] but were also keen observers of the knowledge of the heart.

īmān (A) Absolute, complete, and unshakable faith, certitude, and determination that God alone exists; the complete acceptance of the heart that God is One.

Īmān-Islām (A) The state of the spotlessly pure heart which contains Allah's Holy Qur'an, His divine radiance, His divine wisdom, His truth, His prophets, His angels, and His laws.

When the resplendence of Allah is seen as the completeness within this pure heart of man, that is *Īmān-Islām.* When the complete, unshakable faith of this pure heart is directed toward the One who is completeness and is made to merge with that One; when that heart trusts only in Him and worships only Him, accepting Him as the only perfection and the only One worthy of worship—that is *Īmān-Islām.*

insān (A) True man; a true human being; the true form of man; the form of Allah's qualities, actions, conduct, behavior, and virtues. One who has the completeness of this form and has filled himself with these qualities is an *insān.*

insān kāmil (A) Perfect man, God-realized being. One who has realized Allah as his only wealth, cutting away all the wealth of the world.

in shā'a Allāh (A) If God has willed.

ittiḥād (A) Unity.

jāhil (A) Ignorant; ignorant one.

jihād (A) Holy war. The greater *jihād* or religious war is waged by the believer against his evil desires and bad qualities. The external *jihād,* prescribed by the *sharī'ah* for the repulsion of oppressors, must be conducted under a truly righteous *imām* within rigid restrictions and may be continued only to the limit of what is needed to repel the aggressors.

jum'ah (A) The traditional gathering for prayers on Friday.

juz' (A) Portion; section.

Ka'bah (A) In Islam, the *Ka'bah* is the most important shrine for worship. The place where the earlier prophets and the Final Prophet, Muhammad, gathered together in prayer. On the path of *sharī'ah,* one of the five obligations, or *furūḍ,* is the pilgrimage to the *Ka'bah,* known as *ḥajj.*

Another meaning: the innermost heart, or *qalb,* which is the original source of prayer; the place where a true man, or *insān,* meets Allah face to face. Whoever brings his heart to that state of perfection and prays to God from that heart will be praying from the *Ka'bah.*

kāfir (A) One who rejects faith in Allah or who is ungrateful for the blessings of Allah.

kalimah (A) Affirmation of faith. *Lā ilāh illā Allāh:* There is nothing other than You, O God. Only You are Allah.

The recitation or remembrance of God which cuts away the influence of the five elements (earth, fire, water, air, and ether), washes away all the karma that has accumulated from the very beginning until now, dispels the darkness, beautifies the heart, and causes it to resplend.

The *kalimah* washes the body and the heart of man and makes them pure, makes his wisdom emerge, and impels that wisdom to know the self and God. Lit.: the word. See also: *dhikr, lā ilāh illā Allāh.*

khayr (A) That which is right or good; that which is acceptable to wisdom and to Allah, as opposed to *sharr,* that which is evil or bad.

kufr (A) The rejection of faith in Allah after understanding the truth. Disbelieving in Allah, the *Rasūl,* and the Qur'an; infidelity. Lit.: that which covers the truth. Also means ingratitude.

kursī (A) The gnostic eye; the eye of light; the center of the forehead where the light of Allah's *Nūr,* His resplendence, was impressed on Adam's forehead. Lit.: the seat of the resplendence of Allah.

Lā ilāh illā Allāh (A) There is nothing other than You, O God. Only You are Allah. There is only one Lord, one deity, one God. To accept this with certitude, to strengthen one's *īmān,* or absolute faith, and to affirm this *kalimah* is the state of Islam.

There are two aspects. *Lā ilāh* is the manifestations of creation, or *ṣifāt. Illā Allāh* is the essence, or *dhāt.* All that has appeared, all creation, belongs to *lā ilāh.* The One who created all that, His name is Allah. See also: *kalimah, dhikr.*

Lā ilāh illā Allāh Muḥammad Rasūl Allāh (A) There is nothing other than You, O God. Only You are Allah and Muhammad is the Messenger of God.

lām (A) The Arabic letter (ل) which correlates to the English consonant 'l'. In the transformed man of wisdom, *lām* represents the *Nūr,* the resplendence of Allah. See also: *alif, mīm.*

la'nat al-jahannam (A) The curse of hell.

maghrib (A) The fourth *waqt* of the five-times prayer in Islam. Lit.: the time of sunset; also means the west.

mā shā'a Allāh (A) Whatever God has willed.

al-mawlá (A) The lord; master.

mawlá al-Islām (A) Friends of Islam; master (lord) of Islam.

mawlāwi (A) A sheikh; a teacher; master.

māyā (T) Illusion; the unreality of the visible world; the glitters seen in the darkness of illusion; the 105 million glitters seen in the darkness of the mind which result in 105 million rebirths. Maya is an energy, or *sakti,* which takes on various shapes, causes man to forfeit his wisdom, and confuses and hypnotizes him into a state of torpor. Maya can take many, many millions of hypnotic forms. If man tries to grasp one of these forms with his intellect, though he sees the form he will never catch it, for it will take on yet another form.

mīm (A) The Arabic letter (م) which correlates to the English consonant 'm'. In the transformed man of wisdom, *mīm* represents Muhammad. The shape of *mīm* is like a sperm and from this comes the *nuqṭah,* or dot, which is the form of the world. See also: *alif, lām.*

mi'rāj (A) The night journey of the Prophet Muhammad through the heavens said to have taken place in the twelfth year of the Prophet's mission, on the 27th of the month of *Rajab.* During this event the divine order for five-times prayer was given. Lit.: an ascent.

miskīn (A) A poor person; one who possesses no property at all.

mubārakāt (A) Blessings; the supreme, imperishable treasure of all three worlds (*al-awwal, dunyā,* and *al-ākhirah*).

Muḥaiyaddeen or *Muḥyiddīn* (A) The pure resplendence called the *Quṭb.* The one who manifests the wisdom which lies hidden and buried under illusion (maya). The one who gives life to that wisdom and shows it again as a resplendence. The one who revives the life of wisdom and gives it to someone else. *Muḥaiyaddeen: Mu* is that which existed earlier; *ḥayy* is life, *yā* is a title of greatness, a title of praise; and *dīn* means the light which is perfectly pure. *Dīn* is what existed in the beginning, the 'ancient thing' which was with God originally and is always with Him. To that purity God gave the name *Muḥaiyaddeen. Muḥaiyaddeen* is that beauty which manifested from Allah and to which Allah gave His *wilāyāt* [powers]. Lit.: the giver of life to the true belief.

muham (T) Face or countenance. Muhammad can be defined as the beauty of the heart [*aham*] reflected in the face.

Muḥammad al-Ummī: The unlettered Muhammad.

Muḥammad Muṣṭafá al-Rasūl (A) *Muṣṭafá*—the chosen one; *al-Rasūl*—the Messenger. A name used for Prophet Muhammad.

mu'min (A) A true believer; one of true *īmān,* or absolute faith, certitude, and determination.

Muṣṭafá al-Rasūl (A) The chosen Messenger.

nafs or *nafs ammārah* (A) The seven kinds of base desires. That is, desires meant to satisfy one's own pleasure and comforts. All thoughts are contained within the *ammarāh*. *Ammarāh* is like the mother while the *nafs* are like the children. Lit.: person; spirit; inclination or desire which goads or incites toward evil.

Nūr (A) Light; resplendence of Allah; the plenitude of the light of Allah which has the brilliance of a hundred million suns; the completeness of Allah's qualities. When the plenitude of all these becomes one and resplends as one, that is the *Nūr*—that is Allah's qualities and His beauty. It is the resplendent wisdom which is innate in man and can be awakened.

Nūr Muḥammad (A) The beauty of the qualities and actions of the *wilāyāt* [powers] of Allah, the radiance of Allah's essence, or *dhāt,* which shines within the resplendence of His truth. It was the light of Muhammad called *Nūr Muḥammad* that was impressed upon the forehead of Adam. Of the nine aspects of Muhammad, *Nūr Muḥammad* is that aspect which is the wisdom.

qalam (A) The pen with which God is said to have prerecorded the actions of men. The Prophet said the first thing which God created was the pen [*qalam*] and that it wrote down the quantity of every individual thing to be created, all that was and all that will be to all eternity. Lit.: a reed pen.

qalb (A) The heart within the heart of man; the innermost heart. There are two states for the *qalb*. One state is made up of four chambers which are earth, fire, air, and water, representing Hinduism, Fire Worship, Christianity, and Islam. Inside these four chambers there is a flower, the flower of the *qalb,* which is the divine qualities of God. That is the second state, the flower of grace or *raḥmah*. God's fragrance only exists within this inner *qalb*.

qiblah (A) The direction one faces in prayer. For Jews, the *qiblah* is Jerusalem; for Muslims, it is Mecca. Internally, it is the throne of God within the heart [*qalb*].

Qiyāmah (A) The standing forth; the Day of Reckoning.

qudrah (A) The power of God's grace and the qualities which control all other forces.

Quraysh (A) Name of the tribe in Mecca into which Prophet Muhammad was born.

qurbān (A) Externally, it is a ritual method for the slaughter of animals to purify them and make them permissible, or *ḥalāl,* to eat. Inwardly, it is to sacrifice one's life to the devotion and service of God and to cut away the beastly qualities within the heart of man that cause him to want to slaughter animals.

quṭb (A) Divine analytic wisdom, the wisdom which explains; that which measures the length and breadth of the seven oceans of the *nafs,* or base desires; that which awakens all the truths which have been destroyed and buried in the ocean of maya; that which awakens true *īmān* [absolute faith, certitude, and determination]; that which explains to the *ḥayāh,* to life, the state of purity as it existed in *al-awwal,* the beginning of creation; the grace of the *dhāt,* the essence of God, which awakens the *ḥayāh* of purity and transforms it into the divine vibration.

Quṭb is also a name which has been given to Allah. He can be addressed as *Yā Quṭb* or *Yā Quddūs,* the Holy One. *Quddūs* is His *wilāyah,* His power or miracle, while *Quṭb* is His action. *Wilāyah* is the power of that action. Lit.: axis, axle, pole, pivot. Also, a title used for the great holy men of Islam.

Rabb (A) God; the Lord; the Creator and Protector.

Rabb al-'ālamīn (A) The Ruler of the universes.

al-Raḥīm (A) One of the beautiful ninety-nine names of God—the Most Compassionate.

al-Raḥmān (A) One of the beautiful ninety-nine names of God—the Most Merciful. He is the *Raḥmān.* He is the King. He is the Nourisher, the One who gives food. He is the Compassionate One. He is the One who protects the creations. He is the Beneficent One.

raḥmah (A) God's grace; His benevolence; His wealth. All the good things that we receive from God are called His *raḥmah.* That is the wealth of God's plenitude. If man can receive this, that is very good.

Everything that is within God is *raḥmah,* and if He were to give that grace, it would be an undiminishing, limitless wealth.

raḥmat al-'ālamīn (A) The mercy and compassion of all the universes; the One who gives everything to all His creations.

Rasūl (A) Allah's *Rasūl* is His *dhāt,* that is, the resplendence that emerged from His effulgence, shining radiantly as His Messenger. The manifestation of that resplendence discourses on the explanations of luminous wisdom which he imparts to Allah's creations. He is the one who begs for truth from Allah and intercedes with prayers [*du'ā's*] for all of Allah's creations and for his followers. Therefore Allah has anointed His *Rasūl* with this title: *The Messenger who is the savior for both worlds.* Lit.: the word *rasūl* can be used to refer to any of Allah's apostles or messengers.

Rasūl Allāh (A) Prophet Muhammad, the Messenger of God.

rūḥ (A) The soul; the light ray of God; the light of God's wisdom; *ḥayāh* [life]. Of the six kinds of lives, the soul is the light-life, the ray of the light of *Nūr* [the resplendence of Allah] which does not die. It does not disappear; it is the truth; it exists forever. That is the soul, the light-life.

rukū' (A) A posture in the daily formal *ṣalāh* [prayer] of Islam. A bending over from the torso, with head down and hands resting on knees.

ṣabr (A) Inner patience; to go within patience, to accept it, to think and reflect within it. *Ṣabr* is that patience deep within patience which comforts, soothes, and alleviates mental suffering.

Yā Ṣabūr—one of the ninety-nine names of Allah. God, who in a state of limitless patience is always forgiving the faults of His created beings and continuing to protect them.

saivam (T) Inner purity; in common usage it refers to vegetarianism.

sajdah (A) In the formal prayer of Islam, [*ṣalāh*], a position of prostration on hands and knees, with forehead touching the ground.

ṣalāh (A) Blessing; ritual prayer.

salām (A) The peace of God. Greetings! There are many meanings to the world *salām*. When we say *al-salām,* it means in God's name or in the presence of God, both of us become one without any division; both of us are in a state of unity, a state of peace.

al-salām 'alaykum (A) "May the peace and peacefulness of Allah be upon you." This is the greeting of love. *Al-salām 'alaykum; wa 'alaykum al-salām.* One heart embraces the other with love and greets it with respect and honor. Both hearts are one. In reply, *wa 'alaykum al-salām* means, "May the peace and peacefulness of Allah be upon you also."

al-salām 'alaykum wa-raḥmat Allāh wa-barakātuhu kulluh (A) May all the peace, the beneficence, and the blessings of God be upon you!

ṣalawāt (A) (sing. *ṣalāh*) Prayer; usually used for the supplications asking God to bless the prophets and mankind. See also: *Sallá Allāh 'alayhi wa-sallam.*

Sallá Allāh 'alayhi wa-sallam (A) (pl. *Sallá Allāh 'alayhim wa-sallam*) God bless him and grant him peace. A supplication traditionally spoken after mentioning the name of Prophet Muhammad. The plural form is used when asking God to bless the prophets and mankind.

sawm (A) Fasting.

al-shahādah kalimah (A) The second *kalimah,* the witnessing. *Ashhadu an lā ilāh illā Allāh waḥdahu lā sharīk lahu; wa-ashhadu anna Muḥammad 'abduhu wa-rasūluh*—I witness (testify) that there is no god other than Allah; He is One without partner, and I witness (testify) that Muhammad is His slave and His Messenger. See also: *kalimah,* appendix.

sharr (A) That which is wrong, bad, or evil, as opposed to *khayr* or that which is good.

shukr (A) (pl. *shukūr*) Contentment arising out of gratitude; the state within the inner patience known as *ṣabr;* that which is kept within the treasure chest of patience. Lit.: gratitude; thankfulness.

Yā Shakūr—one of the ninety-nine beautiful names of Allah. To have *shukr* with the help of the One who is *Yā Shakūr* is true *shukr.*

siddhi (T) Magic; miracle; supernatural abilities commonly called miracles and obtained by controlling the elements.

ṣifāt (A) (sing. *ṣifah*) The manifestations of creation; attributes; all that has come to appearance as form.

singhan (T) See: *tārahan, singhan,* and *sūran.*

sirr (A) The secret of Allah.

subḥānahu wa-ta'ālá (A) Glory is His and exaltedness! A spontaneous outpouring of love from a believer's heart upon hearing or uttering the name Allah.

ṣūrah (A) Form or shape, such as the form of man.

sūran (T) See: *tārahan, singhan,* and *sūran.*

ṣūrat al-Ādam (A) Form of Adam.

ṣūrat al-insān (A) The inner form of man. The inner form of man is the Qur'an and is linked together by the twenty-eight letters. This form, this *ṣūrah,* is the *Umm al-Qur'ān,* the source of the Qur'an. It is the Qur'an in which the revelations of Allah are revealed. The sounds in the Qur'an which resonate through wisdom, the Messenger of Allah, Prophet Muhammad, the angels and heavenly beings—all are made to exist in this body as secrets.

takbīr (A) Saying: *"Allāh Akbar."*

tārahan, singhan, and *sūran* (T) The three sons of maya or illusion. *Tārahan* is the trench or the pathway for the sexual act, the birth canal or vagina. *Singhan* is the arrogance present at the moment when the semen is ejaculated (karma). It is the quality of the lion. *Sūran* is the illusory images of the mind enjoyed at the moment of ejaculation. It is all the qualities and energies of the mind.

tasbīḥ (A) The glorification of God.

tawakkul 'alá Allāh (A) Absolute trust and surrender; handing over to God the entire responsibility for everything. Lit.: "Trust in Allah."

tawbah (A) Repentance; asking forgiveness for sins.

tawḥīd (A) The affirmation of the unity of Allah, the principal tenet of Islam.

'ulamā' (A) (sing. *'ālim*) Teachers; learned ones; scholars.

umm (A) Mother.

Umm al-Qur'ān (A) The 'source' or 'mother' of the Qur'an. It is used commonly to refer to the *Sūrat al-Fātiḥah,* or the opening chapter of the Qur'an. It is said that within the 124 letters of the *Sūrat al-Fātiḥah* is contained the meaning of the entire Qur'an. It is often used to denote the eternal source of all the revelations to all of the prophets and is also known as the *Umm al-Kitāb* [the mother, or source of the book]. This is a divine, indestructible tablet on which all is recorded. This is the silent Qur'an which exists as a mystery within the heart [*qalb*] of each person.

ummī (A) One who is unlearned, illiterate. A title given to Muhammad and found in *Sūrah* VIII of the Holy Qur'an.

waḥy (A) Revelation; inspiration from God; the inspired word of God revealed to a prophet; the commandments or words of God. *Waḥys,* or revelations, have come to Adam, Moses, and various other prophets, but most of all to Prophet Muhammad. Muhammad received 6,666 revelations. The histories of each of the prophets were contained within the revelations given to Prophet Muhammad.

waqt (A) Time of prayer. In the religion of Islam there are five specified *waqts,* or times of prayer, each day. But truly, there is only one *waqt.* That is the prayer that never ends, where one is in direct communication with God and one is merged in God.

wilāyah (A) (pl. *wilāyāt*) God's power; that which has been revealed and manifested through God's actions; the miraculous names and actions of God. See also: *Asmā' al-ḥusná.*

zakāh (A) True charity.

Index

Passim denotes that the references are scattered throughout the pages indicated (e.g. 102-107 *passim*).

Judaism, 37-40 *passim*, 12-20 *passim*, 23
Judgment, 68-69, 78
Judgment Day, 19, 55, 62, 116
and Qur'an, 138
and the seventy-three groups, 58-59
fear of, 67
suffering on, 41
see also Day of Questioning
Justice, 9, 21, 27-29, 33-34, 59, 79-80
four kinds, 121-122

Ka'bah, 61, 91
Kalimah(s), 103-104, 107, 125-128, 142
affirm—, 45-47, 90, 130, 138
five—, 125, 143-144
of prophets, 31
al-shahādah, 113-122
sign of Allah, 46
taught by 'Alī, 82-83
taught by Muhammad, 61-62, 91, 117, 119
unites elements, 99-101
Karma, 41, 48, 57, 85, 121, 134
al-Khaṭṭāb, 'Umar Ibn; *see* 'Umar Ibn al-Khaṭṭāb
Khayr; see Goodness
Killing, 63, 70, 80-86, 114-119 *passim*
see also Attacking others; Ritual sacrifice
Kingdom; *see* Allah, kingdom of
Knowledge, divine; *see* Divine knowledge

Language(s), 103-105 *passim*
Life
aim of, 7-9, 24, 70, 108
eternal—, 84, 95
Light, 38, 85, 103-104, 129
of Allah; *see* Allah, light of
of faith, 70, 121
of Islam, 30, 109, 121, 129-130
of Muhammad; *see* Muhammad, light of
of wisdom, 129
within Adam, 46
within innermost heart, 38, 61, 68, 102, 104, 109, 136-137
within man, 46, 50-51, 68, 109
see also Innermost heart, light within
Light form, 41-42
Love, 2, 104, 114-117 *passim*
is Islam, 70
transforms hearts, 92-93, 103, 122, 138
true—, 120
your neighbor, 114-122 *passim*
within innermost heart, 70

Mālik, Ḥabīb Ibn; *see* Ḥabīb Ibn Mālik
Man
creation of, 46-47, 103, 134-136 *passim*
destruction of, 7
light within, 46, 50-51, 68, 109
ninety-six powers of, 102
true—, 2, 38-42, 78-79, 102-103, 137
value of; *see* Life, purpose of
see also Human being
Meat; *see* Ritual sacrifice
Mecca, 58-61, 84, 113
people of, 76, 91
Medina, 58, 61, 75, 91
Mīm, meaning of, 134, 136
Mind, 47, 50, 109, 127
Mirror of heart, 109
Moses, 12, 136
Muhammad, 72, 113, 136-137
aḥmad within, 101, 133, 137
Allah's chosen Messenger, 70
and Moses, 136
and the Qur'an, 78-79, 89, 133-138
companions of, 75-81 *passim,* 83, 86
direct revelation to, 65, 75-82, 136
during holy war, 75-84
final message of, 60
final teaching of, 57
light of, 46, 61, 68, 71, 99-102, 133, 136-137
muham within, 102, 136
nine names of, 101

Ritual sacrifice, 77, 118-119, 134
Russia, 90

Sacrifice, ritual; *see* Ritual sacrifice
Satan, 22, 61, 64, 69, 71, 103
  fall of, 46, 47
Satanic qualities; *see* Qualities, evil
Scriptures, 32, 38-40
Seventy-three groups, 48, 57-59, 115
Sharr; see evil
Signs of Allah, 46
Slave of Allah; *see* Allah, slave of
Slavery, 3, 22
Soul, 50, 129
  see also Light within man
Story, traditional; *see* Traditional story
Suffering, 3, 22, 41, 46, 58, 93-94, 107
Sufis, 59, 136-137
Surrender, 107
  to Allah, 3, 69, 71, 93, 127
  see also Patience, contentment, surrender, and praise

Text, source of this—, 72, 123
Throne
  of Allah, 59, 68
  of true believer, 63, 68
Torah, 19, 38, 136
Traditional stories of the Prophet, 4, 31, 58-59, 67, 85, 89
  explain revelations, 135
  real meaning of, 33
  sign of Allah, 46
Traditional story
  of 'Alī, 119
  of Muhammad, 30, 67, 119
  of 'Umar Ibn al-Khaṭṭāb, 27-29
  see also Direct revelations
True believers, 2, 34, 63, 68, 70, 101-102
  faith of, 89-95 *passim*
  meaning of, 114-115, 120, 135
  see also Throne of true believer
Truth, 28-29, 37-41, 89-92, 121

Uhud, battle of, 62, 84
'Umar Ibn al-Khaṭṭāb, 14, 27-29, 80
Unbelievers, 60, 91-92
United Nations, message to, 21-33 *passim*
United States, message to, 21-23 *passim*, 90
Unity
  in Islam, 29-34, 90-96, 101, 114-122 *passim*
  in prayer, 90, 107-108
  world—, 20-24, 37-42 *passim*
Unlettered one, 135
'Uthmān, 80

Vengeance, 46-47, 60, 64, 120, 129

War
  holy—,
    history of, 75, 84
    rules of, 81-83
    true—, 2, 45-53, 77-80, 83-86
  waging, 11, 18-24, 60-63, 70-72 129
  waging—within, 2, 48-53, 83-86, 93, 120
    see also Innermost heart, holy war within
Water, 62, 99-101
  see also Elements
Wealth
  of God, 2-3, 34, 69, 90, 95
  of this world, 69, 95
Weapons
  Allah's, 85-86 *passim*
  inner and outer, 59-60
  of Islam, 52, 57, 59-61, 67, 71
  of love, 86
  of war, 84-86, 108
Wisdom, 3-4, 40-41, 59, 128, 142
  and *jihād,* 48
  and the *kalimah*, 47
  as light, 38, 102
  in innermost heart, 59
  qualities of, 28-29
  seven states of, 46
  see also Divine knowledge
Words, go beyond, 105, 107

Other Books by M. R. Bawa Muhaiyaddeen (رضي الله عنه)

Truth & Light: brief explanations

Songs of God's Grace

The Divine Luminous Wisdom That Dispels the Darkness

Wisdom of the Divine (Vols. 1–6)

The Guidebook to the True Secret of the Heart (Vols. 1, 2)

God, His Prophets and His Children

Four Steps to Pure *Iman*

The Wisdom of Man

A Book of God's Love

My Love You My Children: 101 Stories for Children of All Ages

Come to the Secret Garden: Sufi Tales of Wisdom

The Golden Words of a Sufi Sheikh

The Tasty, Economical Cookbook (Vols. 1, 2)

Sheikh and Disciple

Maya Veeram or The Forces of Illusion

Asmā'ul-Husnā: The 99 Beautiful Names of Allah

A Mystical Journey

Questions of Life—Answers of Wisdom (Vols. 1, 2)

Treasures of the Heart: Sufi Stories for Young Children

To Die Before Death: The Sufi Way of Life

A Song of Muhammad (صلى الله عليه وسلم)

Hajj: The Inner Pilgrimage

The Triple Flame: The Inner Secrets of Sufism

The Resonance of Allah: Resplendent Explanations Arising from the *Nūr, Allāh's* Wisdom of Grace

Enough for a Million Years

Why Can't I See the Angels: Children's Questions to a Sufi Saint

The Tree That Fell to the West: Autobiography of a Sufi

Booklets

Gems of Wisdom series:

Vol. 1: The Value of Good Qualities
Vol. 2: Beyond Mind and Desire
Vol. 3: The Innermost Heart
Vol. 4: Come to Prayer

Pamphlets

A Contemporary Sufi Speaks:

To Teenagers and Parents
On the Signs of Destruction
On Peace of Mind
On the True Meaning of Sufism
On Unity: The Legacy of the Prophets
The Meaning of Fellowship
Mind, Desire, and the Billboards of the World

Foreign Language Publications

Ein Zeitgenössischer Sufi Spricht über Inneren Frieden (A Contemporary Sufi Speaks on Peace of Mind—German translation)

Deux Discours tirés du Livre L'Islam et la Paix Mondiale: Explications d'un Soufi (Two Discourses from the Book, Islam and World Peace: Explanations of a Sufi—French translation)

¿Quién es Dios? Una explication por el Sheikh Sufi (Who is God? An Explanation by the Sufi Sheikh—Spanish translation)

About the Bawa Muhaiyaddeen Fellowship

Muhammad Raheem Bawa Muhaiyaddeen ㉿, a Sufi mystic from Sri Lanka, was a man of extraordinary wisdom and compassion. For over seventy years he shared his knowledge and experience with people of every race and religion and from all walks of life.

The central branch of The Bawa Muhaiyaddeen Fellowship is in Philadelphia, Pennsylvania, which was M. R. Bawa Muhaiyaddeen's home ㉿ when he lived in the United States before his death in December, 1986. The Fellowship continues to serve as a meeting house, as a reservoir of people and materials for everyone who is interested in his teachings.

The Mosque of Shaikh Muhammad Raheem Bawa Muhaiyaddeen is located on the same property; here the five daily prayers and Friday congregational prayers are observed. An hour west of the Fellowship is the *Mazār,* the tomb of M. R. Bawa Muhaiyaddeen ㉿ which is open daily between sunrise and sunset.

For further information write or phone:

The Bawa Muhaiyaddeen Fellowship
5820 Overbrook Avenue
Philadelphia, Pennsylvania 19131

(215) 879-6300

E-mail Address: info@bmf.org
Web Address: http://www.bmf.org

If you would like to visit the Fellowship, or to obtain a schedule of current events, branch locations and meetings, please write, phone or E-mail *Attn: Visitor Information.*